The Camper's Companion

Tips and Tales
e Trail

"I'd ake up in the middle of nowhere
than in any city on earth."
-Steve McQueen

EDITED BY
ROBERT C. ETHEREDGE

MIRAVISTA PRESS

PUBLISHED BY MIRAVISTA PRESS

ISBN 0-966580-41-9

Library of Congress Catalog Card Number: 2004115026

MiraVista Press
P.O. Box 961
Orinda, CA 94563
888-811-0746
925-253-9472
Fax: 925-940-9516
Email: poetry@miravista.com
Web: http://www.miravista.com

Printed in the United States of America.

INTRODUCTION

Since publishing the hardback anthology *Poetry for a Lifetime* several years ago, I have missed having it with me when I go camping, since it is too heavy to take in my backpack. There have been many times by the campfire that I wish I could read *The Cremation of Sam McGee* or *The Men that Don't Fit In*. Being outdoors is a perfect place to read and reread these classic poems, and even try to memorize some. So, I needed a lightweight book containing the classic poems.

Then, there were all those nights spent staring at the stars trying to remember the constellations, or time spent during thunderstorms trying to remember if I should lay down or crouch down. There were arguments around the campfire about how long water had to be boiled to be safe. For these and similar reasons, I wanted a book with helpful tips that I could refer to on the trail when I needed them.

Next, I felt there were a few classic adventure and survival stories that could be read again and again, and were certainly not to be missed for the first time. I think *To Build a Fire* is the ultimate outdoors tale, while Shackleton's *South* is an almost unbelievable tale of endurance, courage and leadership. Reading these stories makes any of your current problems, like being a little cold, wet, tired or hungry, seem truly insignificant. I was also lucky enough to find the classic story, *Leiningen Versus the Ants,* that I remember listening to around a campfire at Scout camp when I was a boy.

It is for these reasons that I put together this light-in-weight but heavy-in-content collection called *The Camper's Companion*. I tried to fill every page with information that is helpful on the trail. It is not meant to be a read-at-home-before-the-trip book. I hope it will be a lifetime addition to your backpack.

DEDICATION

This book is dedicated to my father, Samuel N. Etheredge, who instilled in me a love of poetry, integrity and patriotism, and edited our first book, *Poetry for a Lifetime*; to my wife, Cheri, for her constant and unwavering support for me over the years; to my children, Parker and Kelsey, who have shared the outdoors with me and hopefully will inherit a love of poetry as well; to my Bernese Mountain Dog, Kayla, who has loved sharing nights with me under the stars; to my two good friends and unbeatable camping companions, Richard and Peter; and to the great outdoors itself which is always the best place to read poetry.

Table of Contents

Tips

POEMS

POEMS

Taken at the Flood
by William Shakespeare in "Julius Caesar"

There is a tide in the affairs of men
Which, taken at the flood, leads on to fortune;
Omitted, all the voyage of their life
Is bound in shallows and in miseries.
On such a full sea are we now afloat,
And we must take the current when it serves,
Or lose our ventures.

Can't
by Edgar Guest

Can't is the worst word that's written or spoken;
  Doing more harm here than slander and lies;
On it is many a strong spirit broken,
  And with it many a good purpose dies.
It springs from the lips of the thoughtless each morning
  And robs us of courage we need through the day:
It rings in our ears like a timely sent warning
  And laughs when we falter and fall by the way.

Can't is the father of feeble endeavor,
  The parent of terror and halfhearted work;
It weakens the efforts of artisans clever,
  And makes of the toiler an indolent shirk.
It poisons the soul of the man with a vision,
  It stifles in infancy many a plan;
It greets honest toiling with open derision
  And mocks at the hopes and the dreams of a man.

Can't is a word none should speak without blushing;
  To utter it should be a symbol of shame;
Ambition and courage it daily is crushing;
  It blights a man's purpose and shortens his aim.
Despise it with all of your hatred of error;
  Refuse it the lodgment it seeks in your brain;
Arm against it as a creature of terror,
  And all that you dream of, you someday shall gain.

Count That Day Lost
by George Eliot

If you sit down at set of sun
And count the acts that you have done,
And, counting, find
One self denying deed, one word
That eased the heart of him who heard,
One glance most kind
Then you may count that day well spent.

But if, through all the livelong day,
You've cheered no heart, by yea or nay—
If, through it all
You've nothing done that you can trace
That brought the sunshine to one face—
No act most small
That helped some soul and nothing cost—
Then count that day as worse than lost.

Charity
by Unknown

There is so much good in the worst of us,
And so much bad in the best of us,
That it ill behooves any of us
To find fault with the rest of us.

TIPS FOR THE TRAIL

What to Do...If You Are Lost

- Stay calm.
- It is usually better to stay in one place. Don't get more lost by wandering around. People will be looking for you at some point--so don't waste energy hiking around.
- Only if no one knows where you are, or if you have people requiring medical assistance of some kind, should you consider trying to walk out.
- Build your shelter, start a fire and collect water as soon as possible. Stay as warm and dry as possible.
- Administer any first aid that is required.
- Attempt to signal periodically. This may involve making sounds with a whistle, building a smoky fire or writing a large message in the snow. The sunlight from mirrors can be seen a long distance so keep trying that.
- If you leave camp, leave a note or sign indicating the direction taken. Mark your trail so you can come back.

O Captain! My Captain!
By Walt Whitman

The tragic assassination of President Abraham Lincoln, "My Captain", inspired Walt Whitman to write this poem.

O Captain! my Captain! our fearful trip is done;
The ship has weather'd every rack, the prize we sought is won;
The port is near, the bells I hear, the people all exulting,
While follow eyes the steady keel, the vessel grim and daring:

But O heart! heart! heart!
O the bleeding drops of red,
Where on the deck my Captain lies,
Fallen cold and dead.

O Captain! my Captain! rise up and hear the bells;
Rise up—for you the flag is flung—for you the bugle trills;
For you bouquets and ribbon'd wreaths for you the shores a-crowding;
For you they call, the swaying mass, their eager faces turning:

Here Captain! dear father!
This arm beneath your head;
It is some dream that on the deck
You've fallen cold and dead.

My Captain does not answer, his lips are pale and still;
My father does not feel my arm, he has no pulse or will;
The ship is anchor'd safe and sound, its voyage closed and done;
From fearful trip the victor ship comes in with object won:

Exult, O shores, and ring, O bells!
But I, with mournful tread,
Walk the deck my Captain lies,
Fallen cold and dead.

TIPS FOR THE TRAIL

First Aid - Hypothermia (drop in body temp)

- To avoid problems in the first place; stay dry and warm, eat well and exercise.
- Get victim to a dry, warm place out of wind.
- Put dry clothes on.
- Get in sleeping bag with another person if possible. Place bottles of hot water into sleeping bag.
- Give warm drinks but no alcohol and avoid caffeine.

Do It Now
by Berton Braley

If with pleasure you are viewing any work a man is doing,
If you like him or you love him, tell him now;
Don't withhold your approbation till the parson makes oration
And he lies with snowy lilies on his brow.
No matter how you shout it, he won't really care about it.
He won't know how many teardrops you have shed;
If you think some praise is due him, now's the time to slip it to him,
For he cannot read his tombstone when he's dead.

More than fame, and more than money, is the comment kind and sunny,
And the hearty, warm approval of a friend.
For it gives to life a savor, and it makes you stronger, braver,
And it gives you heart and spirit to the end.
If he earns your praise—bestow it; if you like him let him know it;
Let the words of true encouragement be said;
Do not wait till life is over and he's underneath the clover,
For he cannot read his tombstone when he's dead.

TIPS FOR THE TRAIL

Survival - Using a Solar Still to Get Water

You never want to drink salt water or urine. But you can distill these liquids, or get water from moist ground and cut vegetation, by using a solar still. Dig a hole in the ground, preferably in moist ground, where the sun will shine. You can place cut vegetation, urine or salt water in the hole as well. Place a cup or bowl in the middle of the hole. Then, cover the hole with a piece of plastic, weighted in the middle over the container. As the sun evaporates the moisture in the hole, distilled water will condense on the plastic and run down into the container.

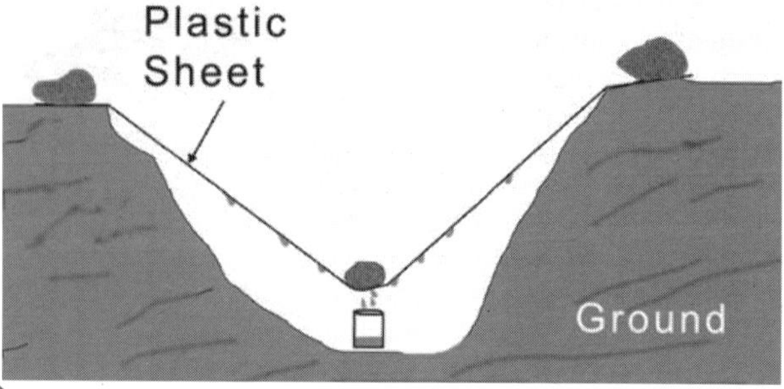

Don't Quit
by Unknown

When things go wrong, as they sometimes will,
When the road you're trudging seems all up hill,
When the funds are low and the debts are high,
And you want to smile, but you have to sigh,
When care is pressing you down a bit,
Rest, if you must—but don't you quit.

Life is queer with its twists and turns,
As everyone of us sometimes learns.
And many a failure turns about
When he might have won had he stuck it out;
Don't give up, though the pace seems slow,
You might succeed with another blow.

Often the goal is nearer than
It seems to a faint and faltering man.
Often the struggler has given up
When he might have captured the victor's cup.
And he learned too late, when the night slipped down,
How close he was to the golden crown.

Success is failure turned inside out—
The silver tint of the clouds of doubt—
And you never can tell how close you are,
It may be near when it seems afar;
So stick to the fight when you're hardest hit—
It's when things seem worst that you mustn't quit.

TIPS FOR THE TRAIL

Survival - Collecting Water Using Plants

If there is vegetation around, you can always attempt to get water by tying a plastic bag over the vegetation and waiting until water condenses inside the bag. The plant roots will be bringing water from deep within the soil. It sure beats trying to dig down by hand.

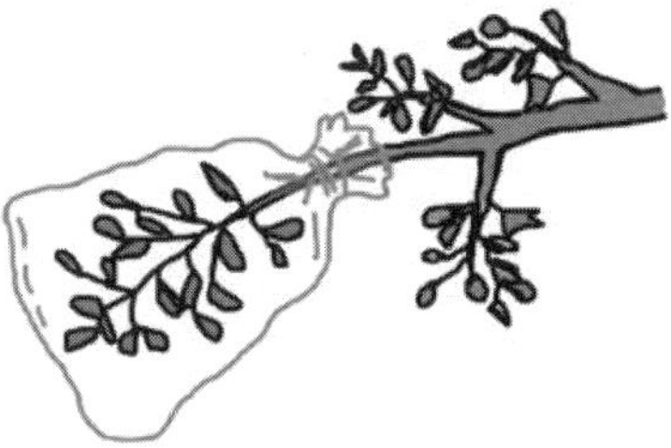

Drop a Pebble in the Water
by James W. Foley

Drop a pebble in the water: just a splash, and it is gone;
But there's half a hundred ripples circling on and on and on,
Spreading, spreading from the center, flowing on out to the sea.
And there is no way of telling where the end is going to be.

Drop a pebble in the water: in a minute you forget,
But there's little waves a flowing, and there's ripples circling yet,
And those little waves a flowing to a great big wave have grown;
You've disturbed a mighty river just by dropping in a stone.

Drop an unkind word, or careless: in a minute it is gone;
But there's half a hundred ripples circling on and on and on.
They keep spreading, spreading, spreading from the center as they go,
And there is no way to stop them, once you've started them to flow.

Drop an unkind word, or careless: in a minute you forget;
But there's little waves a flowing, and there's ripples circling yet,
And perhaps in some sad heart a mighty wave of tears you've stirred,
And disturbed a life was happy, ere you dropped that unkind word.

Drop a word of cheer and kindness: just a flash and it is gone;
But there's half a hundred ripples circling on and on and on,
Bearing hope and joy and comfort on each splashing, dashing wave
Till you wouldn't believe the volume of the one kind word you gave.

Drop a word of cheer and kindness: in a minute you forget;
But there's gladness still a swelling, and there's joy a circling yet,
And you've rolled a wave of comfort whose sweet music can be heard
Over miles and miles of water just by dropping one kind word.

TIPS FOR THE TRAIL

Knots - Two Half Hitches

Used to tie lines to a post or dock eye. It will slide tighter which may be convenient, but it may also slip.

Solitude
by Ella Wheeler Wilcox

Laugh, and the world laughs with you;
Weep, and you weep alone.
For the sad old earth must borrow its mirth,
But has trouble enough of its own.
Sing, and the hills will answer;
Sigh, it is lost on the air.
The echoes bound to a joyful sound,
But shrink from voicing care.

Rejoice, and men will seek you;
Grieve, and they turn and go.
They want full measure of all your pleasure,
But they do not need your woe.
Be glad, and your friends are many;
Be sad, and you lose them all.
There are none to decline your nectared wine,
But alone you must drink life's gall.

Feast, and your halls are crowded;
Fast, and the world goes by.
Succeed and give, and it helps you live,
But no man can help you die.
There is room in the halls of pleasure
For a long and lordly train,
But one by one we must all file on
Through the narrow aisles of pain.

TIPS FOR THE TRAIL

Navigation - Directions from Sun Shadow

You can use the shadow cast by a stick during the day to help determine the East/West direction. This is more effective during the middle of the day. Place a stick around 3 feet tall in the ground as perpendicular as possible (use string and a rock to line it up). Mark the end of the shadow with a rock. Wait 15-30 minutes and place another rock at the end point of the new shadow. A line connecting these two rocks runs approximately East/West.

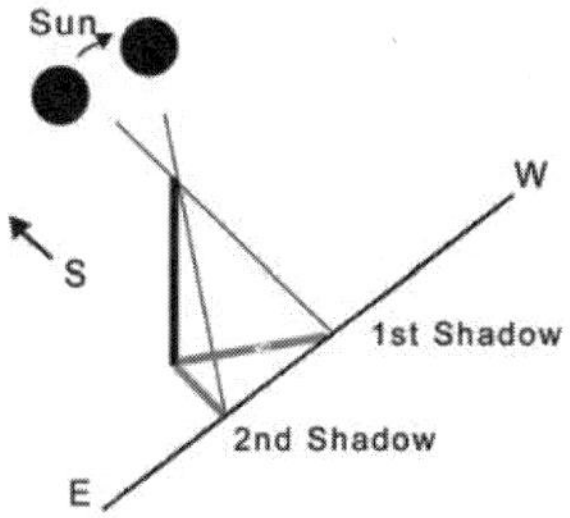

Annabel Lee
by Edgar Allan Poe

It was many and many a year ago,
In a kingdom by the sea,
That a maiden there lived whom you may know
By the name of Annabel Lee;—
And this maiden she lived with no other thought
Than to love and be loved by me.

I was a child and she was a child,
In this kingdom by the sea,
But we loved with a love that was more than love—
I and my Annabel Lee—
With a love that the winged seraphs in Heaven
Coveted her and me.

And this was the reason that, long ago,
In this kingdom by the sea,
A wind blew out of a cloud, chilling
My beautiful Annabel Lee;
So that her high-born kinsmen came
And bore her away from me,
To shut her up in a sepulcher
In this kingdom by the sea.

The angels, not half so happy in Heaven,
Went envying her and me:—
Yes!—that was the reason (as all men know,
In this kingdom by the sea)
That the wind came out of the cloud, by night,
Chilling and killing my Annabel Lee.

But our love it was stronger by far than the love
Of those who were older than we—
Of many far wiser than we—
And neither the angels in Heaven above,
Nor the demons down under the sea,
Can ever dissever my soul from the soul
Of the beautiful Annabel Lee:—

For the moon never beams without bringing me dreams
Of the beautiful Annabel Lee;
And the stars never rise but I feel the bright eyes
Of the beautiful Annabel Lee;
And so, all the night-tide, I lie down by the side
Of my darling,—my darling,—my life and my bride,
In her sepulcher there by the sea—
In her tomb by the sounding sea.

The Sin of Omission
by Margaret E. Sangster

It isn't the thing you do, dear,
  It's the thing you leave undone
That gives you a bit of a heartache
  At setting of the sun.
The tender word forgotten,
  The letter you did not write,
The flowers you did not send, dear,
  Are your haunting ghosts at night.

The stone you might have lifted
  Out of a brother's way;
The bit of heartsome counsel
  You were hurried too much to say;
The loving touch of the hand, dear,
  The gentle, winning tone
Which you had no time nor thought for
  With troubles enough of you own.
Those little acts of kindness
  So easily out of mind,
Those chances to be angels
  Which we poor mortals find—
They come in night and silence,
  Each sad, reproachful wraith,
When hope is faint and flagging,
  And a chill has fallen on faith.

For life is all too short, dear,
  And sorrow is all too great,
To suffer our slow compassion
  That tarries until too late;
And it isn't the thing you do, dear,
  It's the thing you leave undone,
Which gives you a bit of a heartache
  At the setting of the sun.

TIPS FOR THE TRAIL

Navigation - Directions from Constellation Orion

The right hand star in Orion's belt always rises due East and sets due West. It will be easier to determine where it sets as the constellation will be easier to spot and track.

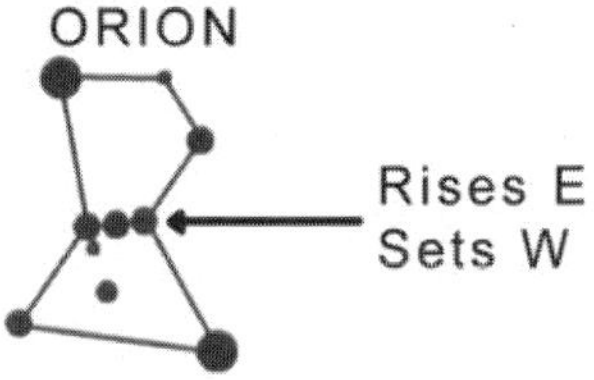

The Winds of Fate
by Ella Wheeler Wilcox

One ship drives east and another drives west
With the selfsame winds that blow.
'Tis the set of the sails
And not the gales
Which tells us the way to go.

Like the winds of the sea are the ways of fate,
As we voyage along through life:
'Tis the set of a soul
That decides its goal,
And not the calm or the strife.

He Who Knows
Persian Proverb

He who knows not, and knows not that he knows not, is a fool,
Shun him;
He who knows not, and knows that he knows not, is a child,
Teach him.
He who knows, and knows not that he knows, is asleep,
Wake him.
He who knows, and knows that he knows, is wise,
Follow him.

TIPS FOR THE TRAIL

What to Do...When Caught by an Avalanche

- Maintain control. Don't panic.
- Shout to members of your group to warn them and let them know where you are.
- Get out of main path of avalanche. You cannot outrun an avalanche which may move more than 50 mph.
- Swim through the snow towards the side of the flow.
- Keep your mouth closed to keep snow out.
- Remove skis, backpacks and other bulky equipment.
- If buried, hold hands in front of face and push out to make breathing space. Move your head from side to side to make a breathing space.
- Don't try to dig out unless you can push one arm into the open air. This effort will only waste your precious air.
- If travelling in avalanche conditions, consider carrying an avalanche beacon to help rescuers.

The Men That Don't Fit In
by Robert Service

There's a race of men that don't fit in,
A race that can't stay still;
So they break the hearts of kith and kin,
And they roam the world at will.
They range the field and they rove the flood,
And they climb the mountain's crest;
Theirs is the curse of the gypsy blood,
And they don't know how to rest.

If they just went straight they might go far;
They are strong and brave and true;
But they're always tired of the things that are,
And they want the strange and new.
They say: "Could I find my proper groove,
What a deep mark I would make!"
So they chop and change, and each fresh move
Is only a fresh mistake.

And each forgets, as he strips and runs
With a brilliant, fitful pace,
It's the steady, quiet, plodding ones
Who win in the lifelong race.
And each forgets that his youth has fled,
Forgets that his prime is past,
Till he stands one day, with a hope that's dead,
In the glare of the truth at last.

He has failed, he has failed; he has missed his chance;
He has just done things by half.
Life's been a jolly good joke on him,
And now is the time to laugh.
Ha, ha! He is one of the Legion Lost;
He was never meant to win;
He's a rolling stone, and it's bred in the bone;
He's a man who won't fit in.

TIPS FOR THE TRAIL

Survival - Distress Signals

- SOS. This is the universal signal for distress. You can send it using sound or lights. The signal is 3 short, 3 long, 3 short (• • • – – – • • •). Or you can write the letters SOS in the snow or with branches.
- Three of anything usually indicates distress: 3 gun shots, 3 whistle blows, 3 fires.

Then Laugh
by Bertha Adams Backus

Build for yourself a strong box,
Fashion each part with care;
When it's strong as your hand can make it
Put all your troubles there;
Hide there all thought of your failures,
And each bitter cup that you quaff;
Lock all your heartaches within it,
Then sit on the lid and laugh.

Tell no one else its contents,
Never its secrets share;
When you've dropped in your care and worry
Keep them forever there;
Hide them from sight so completely
That the world will never dream half;
Fasten the strong box securely—
Then sit on the lid and laugh.

The Man Who Thinks He Can
by Walter D. Wintle

If you think you are beaten, you are;
If you think you dare not, you don't;
If you'd like to win, but think you can't,
It's almost a cinch you won't.
If you think you'll lose, you're lost,
For out in the world we find
Success begins with a fellow's will;
It's all in the state of mind.

If you think you're outclassed, you are;
You've got to think high to rise.
You've got to be sure of yourself before
You can ever win a prize.
Life's battles don't always go
To the stronger or faster man;
But soon or late the man who wins
Is the man who thinks he can.

TIPS FOR THE TRAIL

Navigation - Interesting Fact About the Moon

Did you know that the full moon always rises at sunset? That is because for it to be full, it has to be on the opposite side of the earth from the sun. For similar reasons, crescent moons are always close to the sun, either at dusk or dawn.

The Calf-Path
by Sam Walter Foss

One day, through the primeval wood,
A calf walked home, as good calves should;
But made a trail all bent askew,
A crooked trail as all calves do.
Since then two hundred years have fled,
And, I infer, the calf is dead.
But still he left behind his trail,
And thereby hangs my moral tale.

The trail was taken up next day
By a lone dog that passed that way;
And then a wise bell-wether sheep
Pursued the trail o'er vale and steep,
And drew the flock behind him, too,
As good bell-wethers always do.

And from that day, o'er hill and glade,
Through those old woods a path was made;
And many men wound in and out,
And dodged and turned, and bent about
And uttered words of righteous wrath
Because 'twas such a crooked path.
But still they followed—do not laugh—
The first migrations of that calf,
And through this winding wood-way stalked,
Because he wobbled when he walked.

This forest path became a lane,
That bent, and turned, and turned again;
This crooked lane became a road,
Where many a poor horse with his load
Toiled on beneath the burning sun,
And traveled some three miles in one.
And thus a century and a half
They trod the footsteps of that calf.

The years passed on in swiftness fleet,
The road became a village street;
And this, before men were aware,
A city's crowded thoroughfare;
And soon the central street was this
Of a renowned metropolis;
And men two centuries and a half
Trod in the footsteps of that calf.

Each day a hundred thousand rout
Followed the zigzag calf about;
And o'er his crooked journey went
The traffic of a continent.
A hundred thousand men were led
By one calf near three centuries dead.
They followed still his crooked way,
And lost one hundred years a day;
For thus such reverence is lent
To well-established precedent.

A moral lesson this might teach,
Were I ordained and called to preach:
For men are prone to go it blind
Along the calf-paths of the mind,
And work away from sun to sun
To do what other men have done.
They follow in the beaten track,
And out and in, and forth and back,
And still their devious course pursue,
To keep the path that others do.

But how the wise old wood-gods laugh,
Who saw the first primeval calf!
Ah! many things this tale might teach,—
But I am not ordained to preach.

TIPS FOR THE TRAIL

Navigation - Direction Using the North Star

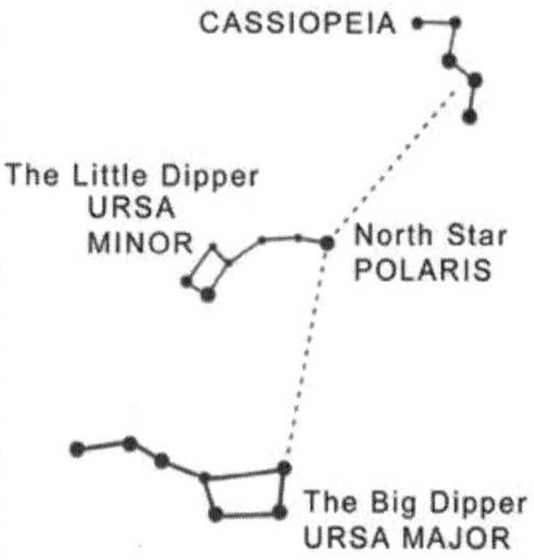

To find North in the Northern Hemisphere, you can always use the North Star. Conveniently, it is always within 1° of North. This is True North, so you have to adjust to Magnetic North, if desired. Draw a line between the last two stars in the bowl of the Big Dipper to point to the North Star, which at times can be very faint. Likewise, if the Big Dipper is hard to see, you can draw a line bisecting the wider opening of the "W" in Cassiopeia and it will also point to the North Star.

The Lord is my Shepherd
Psalms xxiii

The Lord is my shepherd; I shall not want
He maketh me to lie down in green pastures; he leadeth me beside the still waters,
He restoreth my soul; he leadeth me in the paths of righteousness for his name's sake.
Yea, though I walk through the valley of the shadow of death, I will fear no evil; for thou art with me; thy rod and thy staff they comfort me.
Thou preparest a table before me in the presence of mine enemies; thou anointest my head with oil; my cup runneth over.
Surely goodness and mercy shall follow me all the days of my life; and I will dwell in the house of the Lord forever.

Battle Hymn of the Republic
by Julia Ward Howe

Mine eyes have seen the glory of the coming of the Lord:
He is trampling out the vintage where the grapes of wrath are stored;
He hath loosed the fateful lightning of his terrible swift sword:
His truth is marching on.

I have seen him in the watch fires of a hundred circling camps;
They have builded him an altar in the evening dews and damps;
I can read his righteous sentence by the dim and flaring lamps:
His day is marching on.

He has sounded forth the trumpet that shall never call retreat;
He is sifting out the hearts of men before his judgment seat:
O, be swift, my soul, to answer him! be jubilant, my feet!
Our God is marching on.

In the beauty of the lilies Christ was born across the sea,
With a glory in his bosom that transfigures you and me;
As he died to make men holy, let us die to make men free,
While God is marching on.

Crossing the Bar
By Alfred Tennyson

Sunset and evening star,
And one clear call for me,
And may there be no moaning of the bar,
When I put out to sea.

But such a tide as moving seems asleep,
Too full for sound and foam,
When that which drew from out the boundless deep,
Turns again home.

Twilight and evening bell,
And after that the dark!
And may there be no sadness of farewell,
When I embark;

For tho' from out our bourne of time and place,
The flood may bear me far,
I hope to see my Pilot face to face,
When I have crossed the bar.

If I Can Stop One Heart from Breaking
by Emily Dickinson

If I can stop one heart from breaking,
I shall not live in vain;
If I can ease one life the aching,
Or cool one pain,
Or help one fainting robin
Unto his nest again,
I shall not live in vain.

TIPS FOR THE TRAIL

Navigation - Determining Angles with Your Hand

You may need to determine the angular distance between objects in the sky and the horizon. Hold your hand at arms length and use these measurements:

Sun/Moon Diameter	= .5°	(don't look at sun)
Pinky Finger	= 1.5°	
One Finger	= 2°	
Closed Fist	= 10°	
Fist With Thumb Up	= 15°	

How can you use this? Everything in the sky moves 15° every hour (or 1° every 4 minutes) so you can use this to determine how much daylight is left, or help adjust star charts for different times.

Columbus
by Joaquin Miller

Behind him lay the gray Azores,
Behind the Gates of Hercules,
Before him not the ghost of shores,
Before him only shoreless seas.
The good mate said: "Now must we pray,
For lo! the very stars are gone.
Brave Adm'r'l, speak; what shall I say?"
"Why, say: 'Sail on! sail on! and on!'"

"My men grow mutinous day by day;
My men grow ghastly wan and weak."
The stout mate thought of home; a spray
Of salt wave washed his swarthy cheek.
"What shall I say, brave Adm'r'l, say,
If we sight naught but seas at dawn?"
"Why, you shall say, at break of day:
'Sail on! sail on! sail on! and on!'"

They sailed and sailed, as winds might blow,
Until at last the blanched mate said:
"Why, now not even God would know
Should I and all my men fall dead.
These very winds forget their way,
For God from these dread seas is gone.
Now speak, brave Adm'r'l; speak and say"—
He said: "Sail on! sail on! and on!"

They sailed. They sailed. Then spake the mate:
"This mad sea shows his teeth to-night;
He curls his lips, he lies in wait,
With lifted teeth, as if to bite:
Brave Adm'r'l, say but one good word;
What shall we do when hope is gone?"
The words leapt like a leaping sword:
"Sail on! sail on! sail on! and on!"

Then, pale and worn, he kept his deck,
And peered through darkness. Ah, that night
Of all dark nights! And then a speck—
A light! a light! a light! a light!
It grew, a starlit flag unfurled!
It grew to be Time's burst of dawn.
He gained a world; he gave that world
Its grandest lesson: "On! sail on!"

It Couldn't Be Done
by Edgar A. Guest

Somebody said that it couldn't be done,
But he with a chuckle replied
That "maybe it couldn't," but he would be one
Who wouldn't say so till he'd tried.
So he buckled right in with the trace of a grin
On his face. If he worried he hid it.
He started to sing as he tackled the thing
That couldn't be done, and he did it.

Somebody scoffed: "Oh, you'll never do that;
At least no one ever has done it;"
But he took off his coat and he took off his hat,
And the first thing we knew he'd begun it.
With a lift of his chin and a bit of a grin,
Without any doubting or quiddit,
He started to sing as he tackled the thing
That couldn't be done, and he did it.

There are thousands to tell you it cannot be done,
There are thousands to prophesy failure;
There are thousands to point out to you, one by one,
The dangers that wait to assail you.
But just buckle in with a bit of a grin,
Just take off your coat and go to it;
Just start to sing as you tackle the thing
That "cannot be done," and you'll do it.

TIPS FOR THE TRAIL

Survival - Morse Code

A •–	J •–––	S •••	2 ••–––
B –•••	K –•–	T –	3 •••––
C –•–•	L •–••	U ••–	4 ••••–
D –••	M ––	V •••–	5 •••••
E •	N –•	W •––	6 –••••
F ••–•	O –––	X –••–	7 ––•••
G ––•	P •––•	Y –•––	8 –––••
H ••••	Q ––•–	Z ––••	9 ––––•
I ••	R •–•	1 •––––	0 –––––

The Bridge Builder
by Will Allen Dromgoole

An old man, going a lone highway,
    Came at the evening, cold and gray,
To a chasm, vast and deep and wide,
    Through which was flowing a sullen tide.
The old man crossed in the twilight dim—
    That sullen stream had no fears for him;
But he turned, when he reached the other side,
    And built a bridge to span the tide.

"Old man," said a fellow pilgrim near,
    "You are wasting strength in building here.
Your journey will end with the ending day;
    You never again must pass this way.
You have crossed the chasm, deep and wide,
    Why build the bridge at the eventide?"

The builder lifted his old gray head.
    "Good friend, in the path I have come," he said,
"There followeth after me today
    A youth whose feet must pass this way.
This chasm that has been naught to me
    To that fair haired youth may a pitfall be.
He, too, must cross in the twilight dim;
    Good friend, I am building the bridge for him."

TIPS FOR THE TRAIL

Navigation - Direction Using a Watch

You can use your wristwatch as a reverse sundial to help determine South. For digital watches, you will have to picture what a regular watch would look like. This works in the Northern Hemisphere.

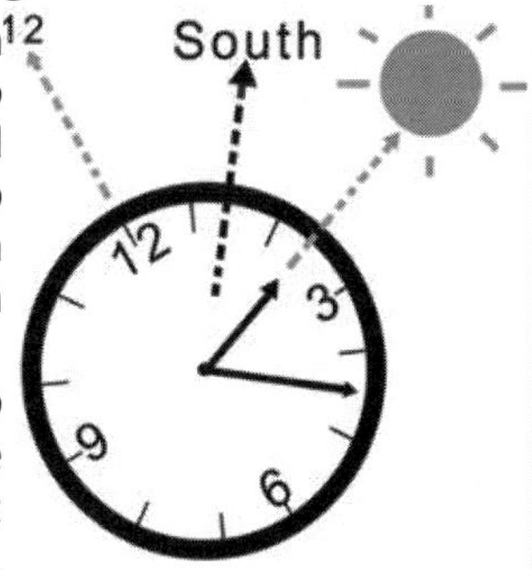

1. Hold your watch parallel to the ground and point the hour hand at the sun (Note: for Daylight Savings Time, subtract one hour from the displayed time to approximate sun time.)
2. With the hour hand pointing at the sun, the direction South will be halfway between the hour hand and 12:00 on your watch.

This is approximate and will not account for your longitude which makes clock time differ from sun time.

Where There's a Will There's a Way
by Eliza Cook

We have faith in old proverbs full surely,
For Wisdom has traced what they tell,
And Truth may be drawn up as purely
From them, as it may from "a well."
Let us question the thinkers and doers,
And hear what they honestly say;
And you'll find they believe, like bold wooers,
In "Where there's a will there's a way."

The hills have been high for man's mounting,
The woods have been dense for his axe,
The stars have been thick for his counting,
The sands have been wide for his tracks.
The sea has been deep for his diving,
The poles have been broad for his sway,
But bravely he's proved in his striving,
That "Where there's a will there's a way."

Have ye vices that ask a destroyer?
Or passions that need your control?
Let Reason become your employer,
And your body be ruled by your soul.
Fight on, though ye bleed in the trial,
Resist with all strength that ye may;
Ye may conquer Sin's host by denial;
For "Where there's a will there's a way."

Have ye Poverty's pinching to cope with?
Does Suffering weigh down your might?
Only call up a spirit to hope with,
And dawn may come out of the night.
Oh! much may be done by defying
The ghosts of Despair and Dismay;
And much may be gained by relying
On "Where there's a will there's a way."

Should ye see afar off that worth winning,
Set out on the journey with trust;
And ne'er heed if your path at beginning
Should be among brambles and dust.
Though it is but by footsteps ye do it.
And hardships may hinder and stay,
Walk with faith, and be sure you'll get through it;
For "Where there's a will there's a way."

A Friend's Greeting
by Edgar A. Guest

I'd like to be the sort of friend that you have been to me;
I'd like to be the help that you've been always glad to be;
I'd like to mean as much to you each minute of the day
As you have meant, old friend of mine, to me along the way.

I'd like to do the big things and the splendid things for you,
To brush the gray from out your skies and leave them only blue;
I'd like to say the kindly things that I so oft have heard,
And feel that I could rouse your soul the way that mine
you've stirred.

I'd like to give back the joy that you have given me,
Yet that were wishing you a need I hope will never be;
I'd like to make you feel as rich as I, who travel on
Undaunted in the darkest hours with you to lean upon.

I'm wishing at this Christmas time that I could but repay
A portion of the gladness that you've strewn along my way;
And could I have one wish this year, this only would it be:
I'd like to be the sort of friend that you have been to me.

TIPS FOR THE TRAIL

Survival - Catching Game for Food

If you are in a survival situation and have to catch game to survive, you can construct a number of traps or deadfalls. Many involve making a snare from heavy line or wire and arranging it near an animal run. Or make a deadfall similar to the following diagram to crush smaller animals (or bigger if you have a big rock but don't crush yourself.) The sticks are arranged so that

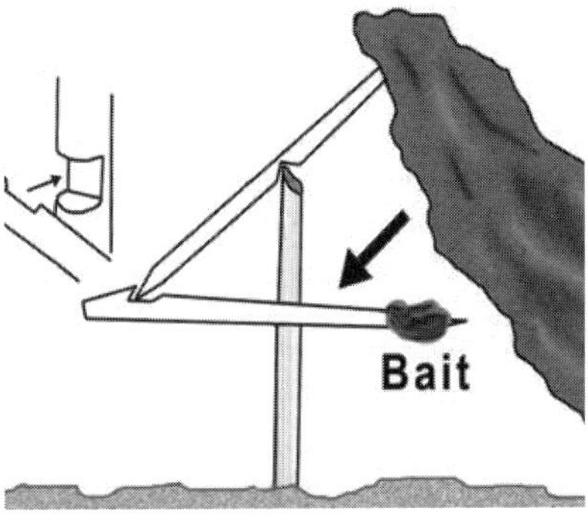

any animal getting the bait will cause the sticks to fall and the rock to release. The bait needs to be selected and placed according to the type of animal.

A Mile with Me
by Henry Van Dyke

O, who will walk a mile with me
Along life's merry way?
A comrade blithe and full of glee,
Who dares to laugh out loud and free,
And let his frolic fancy play,
Like a happy child, through the flowers gay
That fill the field and fringe the way
Where he walks a mile with me.

And who will walk a mile with me
Along life's weary way?
A friend whose heart has eyes to see
The stars shine out o'er the darkening lea,
And the quiet rest at the end o' the day,—
A friend who knows, and dares to say,
The brave, sweet words that cheer the way
Where he walks a mile with me.

With such a comrade, such a friend,
I fain would walk till journey's end,
Through summer sunshine, winter rain,
And then?—Farewell, we shall meet again!

Always Finish
by Unknown

If a task is once begun
Never leave it til it's done.
Be the labor great or small,
Do it well or not at all.

TIPS FOR THE TRAIL

Navigation - Direction at Noon

You can determine South at exactly Noon local time as the sun, in the Northern hemisphere, will always be due South. Remember to adjust for Daylight Savings Time as local Noon will be closer to 1:00pm in that instance. The time of local noon also varies with your longitude. To determine the exact time of local Noon, you must either know ahead of time from a newspaper or other source, or you can use local sunrise and sunset to determine noon. Take the time that the sun rises (upper rim in view) to the time that it sets (sun disappears) and divide that number in two. Then add that number to the sunrise time to get the time of local noon.

IF
by Rudyard Kipling

If you can keep your head when all about you
Are losing theirs and blaming it on you;
If you can trust yourself when all men doubt you,
But make allowance for their doubting too:
If you can wait and not be tired by waiting,
Or, being lied about, don't deal in lies,
Or being hated, don't give way to hating,
And yet don't look too good, nor talk too wise;

If you can dream—and not make dreams your master,
If you can think—and not make thoughts your aim,
If you can meet with Triumph and Disaster
And treat those two impostors just the same:
If you can bear to hear the truth you've spoken
Twisted by knaves to make a trap for fools,
Or watch the things you gave your life to, broken,
And stoop and build 'em up with worn-out tools;

If you can make one heap of all your winnings
And risk it on one turn of pitch-and-toss,
And lose, and start again at your beginnings,
And never breathe a word about your loss:
If you can force your heart and nerve and sinew
To serve your turn long after they are gone,
And so hold on when there is nothing in you
Except the Will which says to them: "Hold on!"

If you can talk with crowds and keep your virtue,
Or walk with Kings—nor lose the common touch,
If neither foes nor loving friends can hurt you,
If all men count with you, but none too much:
If you can fill the unforgiving minute
With sixty seconds' worth of distance run,
Yours is the Earth and everything that's in it,
And—which is more—you'll be a Man, my son!

TIPS FOR THE TRAIL

What To Do...When Caught by Quicksand

- Carry a strong pole when travelling around quicksand. If you get trapped, lay the pole flat and lay on your back on top of it.
- Do not struggle. You will only sink deeper.
- Drop down and try to crawl out. You need to spread your weight out as much as possible.
- Try to lay flat and float out by wriggling your body.
- Don't panic. You can float in quicksand if you relax.

The Things That Haven't Been Done Before
by Edgar Guest

The things that haven't been done before,
Those are the things to try;
Columbus dreamed of an unknown shore
At the rim of the far flung sky,
And his heart was bold and his faith was strong
As he ventured in dangers new,
And he paid no heed to the jeering throng
Or the fears of the doubting crew.

The many will follow the beaten track
With guideposts on the way.
They live and have lived for ages back
With a chart for every day.
Someone has told them it's safe to go
On the road he has traveled o'er,
And all that they ever strive to know
Are the things that were known before.

A few strike out, without map or chart,
Where never a man has been,
From the beaten paths they draw apart
To see what no man has seen.
There are deeds they hunger alone to do;
Though battered and bruised and sore,
They blaze the path for the many, who
Do nothing not done before.

The things that haven't been done before
Are the tasks worthwhile today;
Are you one of the flock that follows, or
Are you one that shall lead the way?
Are you one of the timid souls that quail
At the jeers of a doubting crew,
Or dare you, whether you win or fail,
Strike out for a goal that's new?

TIPS FOR THE TRAIL

Knots - Clinch Knot

This is a perfect knot to tie your hook to your fishing line. Wet the line as you pull it tight.

The Cremation of Sam McGee
by Robert Service

This is a great example of "double rhyming". This is rhyming within each line and at the ends of the line for the entire poem.

There are strange things done in the midnight sun
By the men who moil for gold;
The Arctic trails have their secret tales
That would make your blood run cold;
The Northern Lights have seen queer sights,
But the queerest they ever did see
Was that night on the marge of Lake Lebarge
I cremated Sam McGee.

Now Sam McGee was from Tennessee, where the cotton blooms and blows.
Why he left his home in the South to roam 'round the Pole, God only knows.
He was always cold, but the land of gold seemed to hold him like a spell;
Though he'd often say in his homely way that "he'd sooner live in hell."

On a Christmas Day we were mushing our way over the Dawson trail.
Talk of your cold! through the parka's fold it stabbed like a driven nail.
If our eyes we'd close, then the lashes froze till sometimes we couldn't see;
It wasn't much fun, but the only one to whimper was Sam McGee.

And that very night, as we lay packed tight in our robes beneath the snow,
And the dogs were fed, and the stars o'erhead were dancing heel and toe,
He turned to me, and "Cap," says he, "I'll cash in this trip, I guess;
And if I do, I'm asking that you won't refuse my last request."

Well, he seemed so low that I couldn't say no; then he says with a sort of moan:
"It's the curs'ed cold, and it's got right hold till I'm chilled clean through to the bone.
Yet 'tain't being dead—it's my awful dread of the icy grave that pains;
So I want you to swear that, foul or fair, you'll cremate my last remains."

A pal's last need is a thing to heed, so I swore I would not fail;
And we started on at the streak of dawn; but God! he looked ghastly pale.
He crouched on the sleigh, and he raved all day of his home in Tennessee;
And before nightfall a corpse was all that was left of Sam McGee.

There wasn't a breath in that land of death, and I hurried, horror-driven,
With a corpse half hid that I couldn't get rid, because of a promise given;
It was lashed to the sleigh, and it seemed to say: "You may tax your brawn and brains,
But you promised true, and it's up to you to cremate those last remains."

Now a promise made is a debt unpaid, and the trail has its own stern code.
In the days to come, though my lips were dumb, in my heart how I cursed that load.
In the long, long night, by the lone firelight, while the huskies, round in a ring,
Howled out their woes to the homeless snows—O God! how I loathed the thing.

And every day that quiet clay seemed to heavy and heavier grow;
And on I went, though the dogs were spent and the grub was getting low;
The trail was bad, and I felt half mad, but I swore I would not give in;
And I'd often sing to the hateful thing, and it hearkened with a grin.

Till I came to the marge of Lake Lebarge, and a derelict there lay;
It was jammed in the ice, but I saw in a trice it was called the "Alice May."
And I looked at it, and I thought a bit, and I looked at my frozen chum;
Then "Here, " said I, with a sudden cry, "is my cre-ma-tor-eum."

Some planks I tore from the cabin floor, and I lit the boiler fire;
Some coal I found that was lying around, and I heaped the fuel higher;
The flames just soared, and the furnace roared—such a blaze you seldom see;
And I burrowed a hole in the glowing coal, and I stuffed in Sam McGee.

Then I made a hike, for I didn't like to hear him sizzle so;
And the heavens scowled, and the huskies howled, and the wind began to blow.
It was icy cold, but the hot sweat rolled down my cheeks, and I don't know why;
And the greasy smoke in an inky cloak went streaking down the sky.

I do not know how long in the snow I wrestled with grisly fear;
But the stars came out and they danced about ere again I ventured near;
I was sick with dread, but I bravely said: "I'll just take a peep inside.
I guess he's cooked, and it's time I looked"; ...then the door I opened wide.

And there sat Sam, looking cool and calm, in the heart of the furnace roar;
And he wore a smile you could see a mile, and he said: "Please close that door.
It's fine in here, but I greatly fear you'll let in the cold and storm—
Since I left Plumtree, down in Tennessee, it's the first time I've been warm."

There are strange things done in the midnight sun
By the men who moil for gold;
The Arctic trails have their secret tales
That would make your blood run cold;
The Northern Lights have seen queer sights,
But the queerest they ever did see
Was that night on the marge of Lake Lebarge
I cremated Sam McGee.

Casey At the Bat
by Ernest Lawrence Thayer

The outlook wasn't brilliant for the Mudville nine that day;
The score stood two to four, with but an inning left to play.
So, when Cooney died at second, and Burrows did the same,
A pallor wreathed the features of the patrons of the game.

A straggling few got up to go, leaving there the rest,
With that hope which springs eternal within the human breast.
For they thought: "If only Casey could get a whack at that,"
They'd put even money now, with Casey at the bat.

But Flynn preceded Casey, as did also Jimmy Blake,
And the former was a pudd'n, and the latter was a fake.
So on that stricken multitude a deathlike silence sat;
For there seemed but little chance of Casey's getting to the bat.

But Flynn let drive a "single," to the wonderment of all.
And the much despised Blakey "tore the cover off the ball."
And when the dust had lifted, and they saw what had occurred,
There was Blakey safe at second, and Flynn a huggin' third.

Then from the gladdened multitude went up a joyous yell—
It rumbled in the mountaintops, it rattled in the dell;
It struck upon the hillside and rebounded on the flat;
For Casey, mighty Casey, was advancing to the bat.

There was ease in Casey's manner as he stepped into his place,
There was pride in Casey's bearing and a smile on Casey's face;
And when responding to the cheers he lightly doffed his hat,
No stranger in the crowd could doubt 'twas Casey at the bat.

Ten thousand eyes were on him as he rubbed his hands with dirt,
Five thousand tongues applauded when he wiped them on his shirt;
Then when the writhing pitcher ground the ball into his hip,
Defiance glanced in Casey's eye, a sneer curled Casey's lip.

And now the leather covered sphere came hurtling through the air,
And Casey stood a watching it in haughty grandeur there.
Close by the sturdy batsman the ball unheeded sped;
"That ain't my style," said Casey. "Strike one," the umpire said.

From the benches, black with people, there went up a muffled roar,
Like the beating of the storm waves on the stern and distant shore.
"Kill him! kill the umpire!" shouted someone on the stand;
And it's likely they'd have killed him had not Casey raised his hand.

With a smile of Christian charity great Casey's visage shone;
He stilled the rising tumult, he bade the game go on.
He signaled to the pitcher, and once more the spheroid flew;
But Casey still ignored it, and the umpire said, "Strike two."

"Fraud!" cried the maddened thousands, and the echo answered "Fraud!"
But one scornful look from Casey and the audience was awed;
They saw his face grow stern and cold, they saw his muscles strain,
And they knew that Casey wouldn't let the ball go by again.

The sneer is gone from Casey's lips, his teeth are clenched in hate,
He pounds with cruel vengeance his bat upon the plate;
And now the pitcher holds the ball, and now he lets it go,
And now the air is shattered by the force of Casey's blow.

Oh, somewhere in this favored land the sun is shining bright,
The band is playing somewhere, and somewhere hearts are light;
And somewhere men are laughing, and somewhere children shout,
But there is no joy in Mudville: Mighty Casey has struck out.

TIPS FOR THE TRAIL

First Aid -Hypoxia (lack of Oxygen)

Symptoms

- Increased breathing.
- Dizzy.
- Sleepy.
- Lips/nails turn blue.
- Bad judgement.

Treatment

- Get victim more oxygen by using an O2 bottle.
- Get them to a lower altitude as soon as possible and to medical help if still required.

Woodman, Spare That Tree
by George Perkins Morris

Woodman, spare that tree!
    Touch not a single bough!
In youth it sheltered me,
    And I'll protect it now.
'Twas my forefather's hand
    That placed it near his cot;
There, woodman, let it stand,
    Thy axe shall harm it not!

That old familiar tree,
    Whose glory and renown
Are spread o'er land and sea,
    And wouldst thou hew it down?
Woodman, forbear thy stroke!
    Cut not its earth bound ties;
O, spare that aged oak,
    Now towering to the skies!

When but an idle boy
    I sought its grateful shade;
In all their gushing joy
    Here too my sisters played.
My mother kissed me here;
    My father pressed my hand—
Forgive this foolish tear,
    But let that old oak stand!

My heart strings round thee cling,
    Close as thy bark, old friend!
Here shall the wild bird sing,
    And still thy branches bend.
Old tree! the storm still brave!
    And, woodman, leave the spot;
While I've a hand to save,
    Thy axe shall hurt it not.

TIPS FOR THE TRAIL

Knots - Clove Hitch

Attaches ropes to poles without jamming. May loosen without pressure. Used to start and end lashings.

Trees
by Sergeant Joyce Kilmer

Kilmer was 32 years old, serving with the 165th Infantry in World War I, when he was killed in action in France July 30, 1918.

I think that I shall never see
A poem lovely as a tree.

A tree whose hungry mouth is prest
Against the earth's sweet flowing breast;

A tree that looks at God all day,
And lifts her leafy arms to pray;

A tree that may in Summer wear
A nest of robins in her hair,

Upon whose bosom snow has lain;
Who intimately lives with rain.

Poems are made by fools like me,
But only God can make a tree.

TIPS FOR THE TRAIL

First Aid - Heat Stroke/Exhaustion

It is important to be able to distinguish between heat exhaustion and heat stroke as heat stroke can be fatal.

	Symptoms	Treatment
Heat Exhaustion	Cool, MOIST skin sweating headache dizzy	Give water and salt Put on cool clothing Rest in shade
Heat Stroke	Hot, DRY skin dizzy headache confused rapid breathing rapid pulse unconscious high body temp above 105°F	This is a medical emergency. Lower the body temperature immediately. Move to shade. Remove clothing. Bathe in cool/cold water and fan to increase cooling.

The Raven
by Edgar Allan Poe

Once upon a midnight dreary, while I pondered, weak and weary,
Over many a quaint and curious volume of forgotten lore,
While I nodded, nearly napping, suddenly there came a tapping,
As of someone gently rapping, rapping at my chamber door.
"'Tis some visitor," I muttered, "tapping at my chamber door;
Only this, and nothing more."

Ah, distinctly I remember, it was in the bleak December,
And each separate dying ember wrought its ghost upon the floor.
Eagerly I wished the morrow; vainly I had sought to borrow
From my books surcease of sorrow, sorrow for the lost Lenore,
For the rare and radiant maiden whom the angels name Lenore,
Nameless here forevermore.

And the silken sad uncertain rustling of each purple curtain
Thrilled me—filled me with fantastic terrors never felt before;
So that now, to still the beating of my heart, I stood repeating,
"'Tis some visitor entreating entrance at my chamber door,
Some late visitor entreating entrance at my chamber door
This it is, and nothing more."

Presently my soul grew stronger; hesitating then no longer,
"Sir," said I, "or madam, truly your forgiveness I implore;
But the fact is, I was napping, and so gently you came rapping,
And so faintly you came tapping, tapping at my chamber door,
That I scarce was sure I heard you." Here I opened wide the door;—
Darkness there, and nothing more.

Deep into the darkness peering, long I stood there, wondering, fearing,
Doubting, dreaming dreams no mortals ever dared to dream before;
But the silence was unbroken, and the stillness gave no token,
And the only word there spoken was the whispered word, "Lenore?"
This I whispered, and an echo murmured back the word, "Lenore!"
Merely this, and nothing more.

Back into the chamber turning, all my soul within me burning,
Soon again I heard a tapping, something louder than before,
"Surely," said I, "surely, that is something at my window
lattice
Let me see, then, what thereat is, and this mystery explore;
Let my heart be still a moment, and this mystery explore;
'Tis the wind, and nothing more."

Open-here I flung the shutter, when, with many a flirt and
flutter,
In there stepped a stately raven, of the saintly day of yore.
Not the least obeisance made he; not a minute stopped or
stayed he;
But with mien of lord or lady, perched above my chalice
door;
Perched upon a bust of Pallas, just above my chamber door,
Perched, and sat, and nothing more.

Then this ebony bird beguiling my sad fancy into smiling,
By the grave and stern decorum of the countenance it wore,
"Though thy crest be shorn and shaven, thou," I said, "art
sure no craven,
Ghastly, grim, and ancient raven, wandering from the nightly
shore.
Tell me what thy lordly name is on the Night's Plutonian
shore."
Quoth the raven, "Nevermore."

Much I marvelled this ungainly fowl to hear discourse so
plainly,
Though its answer little meaning, little relevancy bore;
For we cannot help agreeing that no living human being
Ever yet was blessed with seeing bird above his chamber
door,
Bird or beast upon the sculptured bust above his chamber
door,
With such name as "Nevermore."

But the raven, sitting lonely on that placid bust, spoke only
That one word, as if his soul in that one word he did outpour.
Nothing further then he uttered; not a feather then he fluttered;
Till I scarcely more than muttered, "Other friends have flown
before;
On the morrow he will leave me, as my hopes have flown
before."
Then the bird said, "Nevermore."

Startled at the stillness broken by reply so aptly spoken,
"Doubtless," said I, "what it utters is its only stock and store,
Caught from some unhappy master, from unmerciful disaster
Followed fast and followed faster, till his songs one burden bore,—
Till the dirges of his hope that melancholy burden bore
Of Never-nevermore."

But the raven still beguiling all my fancy into smiling,
Straight I wheeled a cushioned seat in front of bird and bust and door;
Then, upon the velvet sinking, I betook myself to linking
Fancy unto fancy, thinking what this ominous bird of yore,
What this grim, ungainly, ghastly, gaunt, and ominous bird of yore
Meant in croaking, "Nevermore."

Thus I sat engaged in guessing, but no syllable expressing
To the fowl, whose fiery eyes now burned into my bosom's core
This and more I sat divining with my head at ease reclining
On the cushion's velvet lining that the lamplight gloated o'er
But whose velvet violet lining with the lamplight gloat'ing o'er
She shall press, ah, nevermore.

Then, methought, the air grew denser, perfumed from an unseen censer
Swung by seraphim whose footfalls tinkled on the tufted floor.
"Wretch," I cried, "thy God hath lent thee—by these angels he hath sent thee
Respite—respite and nepenthe from thy memories of Lenore!
Quaff, O quaff this kind nepenthe, and forget this lost Lenore!"
Quoth the raven, "Nevermore!"

"Prophet!" said I, "thing of evil!—prophet still, if bird or devil!
Whether Tempter sent, or whether tempest tossed thee here ashore,
Desolate, yet all undaunted, on this desert land enchanted
On this home by horror haunted—tell me truly, I implore:
Is there—is there balm in Gilead?—tell me—tell me I implore!"
Quoth the raven, "Nevermore."

"Prophet!" said I, "thing of evil-prophet still, if bird or devil!
By that heaven that bends above us,—by that God we both adore—
Tell this soul with sorrow laden, if, within the distant Aidenn,
It shall clasp a sainted maiden, whom the angels name Lenore—
Clasp a rare and radiant maiden, whom the angels name Lenore?"
Quoth the raven, "Nevermore."

"Be that word our sign of parting, bird or fiend!" I shrieked, upstarting—
"Get thee back into the tempest and the Night's Plutonian shore!
Leave no black plume as a token of that lie thy soul hath spoken!
Leave my loneliness unbroken!—quit the bust above my door!
Take thy beak from out my heart, and take thy form from off my door!"
Quoth the raven, "Nevermore."

And the raven, never flitting, still is sitting, still is sitting
On the pallid bust of Pallas just above my chamber door;
And his eyes have all the seeming of a demon's that is dreaming;
And the lamplight o'er him streaming throws the shadow on the floor;
And my soul from out that shadow that lies floating on the floor
Shall be lifted—nevermore!

TIPS FOR THE TRAIL

What to Do...When Travelling on Ice

Every patch of ice is different due to the conditions surrounding its freezing. While safe in one area, a nearby area may be weaker, particularly if the water is moving beneath the ice. The general guidelines are:

< 3"	- Dangerous
4"	- OK for skating, walking
7"	- OK for snowmobiles
12"	- OK for cars

If in doubt, be careful. Do not walk in groups. Carry a long pole sideways to stop your fall and help you get out.

If You Fall In

- Move around the hole until you find the strongest part, usually where you fell in.
- Put your arms up on the ice (use keys or other sharp object it you have it). Kick your feet like swimming.
- Once out, roll away from the hole. Do not stand up.

How Did You Die
by Edmund Vance Cooke

Did you tackle the trouble that came your way
With a resolute heart and cheerful?
Or hide your face from the light of day
With a craven soul and fearful?
Oh, a trouble's a ton, or a trouble's an ounce,
Or a trouble is what you make it.
And it isn't the fact that you're hurt that counts,
But only how did you take it?

You are beaten to earth? Well, well, what's that?
Come up with a smiling face.
It's nothing against you to fall down flat,
But to lie there—that's disgrace.
The harder you're thrown, why, the higher you bounce;
Be proud of your blackened eye!
It isn't the fact that you're licked that counts;
It's how did you fight—and why?

And though you be done to the death, what then?
If you battled the best you could,
If you played your part in the world of men,
Why, the Critic will call it good.
Death comes with a crawl, or comes with a pounce,
And whether he's slow or spry,
It isn't the fact that you're dead that counts,
But only how did you die?

TIPS FOR THE TRAIL

First Aid - Frostbite

- Get the victim to a warm place.
- Take warm, not hot, bath -- around 102° to 108°F.
- Wrap in warm blanket.
- Don't expose to open fire.
- Don't rub skin or rub with snow.
- Give hot drinks but no alcohol.
- Only thaw out frostbite if you can keep it thawed. If you have to hike back out through snow, wait until you get out to thaw out the body part.
- Get the victim to medical help as soon as possible.

Barbara Frietchie
by John Greenleaf Whittier

During the Civil War, Robert E. Lee and Stonewall Jackson were able to invade the North on only a very few occasions. On one of these trips, this episode was said to have occurred in Frederick, Maryland.

Up from the meadow rich with corn,
Clear in the cool September morn,
The clustered spires of Frederick stand
Green walled by the hills of Maryland.
Round about them orchards sweep,
Apple and peach tree fruited deep,
Fair as the garden of the Lord
To the eyes of the famished rebel horde,
On that pleasant morn of the early fall
When Lee marched over the mountain wall;
Over the mountains winding down,
Horse and foot, into Frederick town.

Forty flags with their silver stars,
Forty flags with their crimson bars,
Flapped in the morning wind: the sun
Of noon looked down, and saw not one.
Up rose old Barbara Frietchie then,
Bowed with her fourscore years and ten;
Bravest of all in Frederick town,
She took up the flag the men hauled down;
In her attic window the staff she set,
To show that one heart was loyal yet.

Up the street came the rebel tread,
Stonewall Jackson riding ahead.
Under his slouched hat left and right
He glanced; the old flag met his sight.
"Halt"—the dust brown ranks stood fast.
"Fire"—out blazed the rifle blast.
It shivered the window, pane and sash;
It rent the banner with seam and gash.
Quick, as it fell, from the broken staff
Dame Barbara snatched the silken scarf.
She leaned far out on the windowsill,
And shook it forth with a royal will.
"Shoot, if you must, this old gray head,
But spare your country's flag," she said.

A shade of sadness, a blush of shame,
Over the face of the leader came;
The nobler nature within him stirred
To life at that woman's deed and word;
"Who touches a hair on yon gray head
Dies like a dog! March on!" he said.
All day long through Frederick street
Sounded the tread of marching feet:
All day long that free flag tossed
Over the heads of the rebel host.
Ever its torn folds rose and fell
On the loyal winds that loved it well;
And through the hill gaps sunset light
Shone over it with a warm good night.

Barbara Frietchie's work is o'er,
And the Rebel rides on his raids no more.
Honor to her! and let a tear
Fall, for her sake, on Stonewall's bier.
Over Barbara Frietchie's grave
Flag of Freedom and Union, wave!
Peace and order and beauty draw
Round thy symbol of light and law;
And ever the stars above look down
On thy stars below in Frederick town!

TIPS FOR THE TRAIL

First Aid - Removing a Fish Hook

- If the hook is barbed and deeply embedded, consider pushing it all the way through and snipping the barb off before removing.
- Hooks that are not too deeply embedded may be removed using a piece of string or line to help pull the hook out. After wrapping the string around the hook as shown, press down on the hook to push the barb down while pulling on the string in the direction shown.
- Clean all open wounds and treat with an antibiotic.
- If the opening is deep, seek medical assistance as soon as possible.

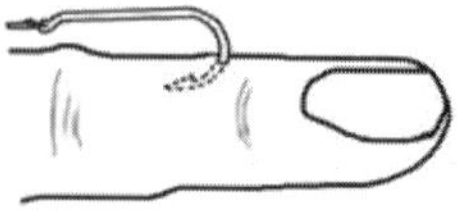
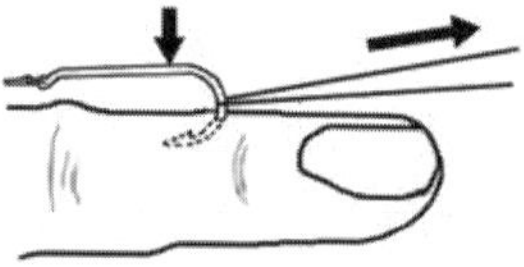

The Declaration of Independence
by Thomas Jefferson, July 4, 1776

When in the Course of human events, it becomes necessary for one people to dissolve the political bands which have connected them with another, and to assume, among the Powers of the earth, the separate and equal station to which the Laws of Nature and of Nature's God entitle them, a decent respect to the opinions of mankind requires that they should declare the causes which impel them to the separation.

We hold these truths to be self-evident, that all men are created equal, that they are endowed by their Creator with certain unalienable Rights, that among these are Life, Liberty, and the pursuit of Happiness. That to secure these rights, Governments are instituted among Men, deriving their just powers from the consent of the governed, That whenever any Form of Government becomes destructive of these ends, it is the Right of the People to alter or to abolish it, and to institute new Government, laying its foundation on such principles and organizing its powers in such form, as to them shall seem most likely to effect their Safety and Happiness. Prudence, indeed, will dictate that Governments long established should not be changed for light and transient causes; and accordingly all experience hath shown, that mankind are more disposed to suffer, while evils are sufferable, than to right themselves by abolishing the forms to which they are accustomed. But when a long train of abuses and usurpations, pursuing invariably the same Object evinces a design to reduce them under absolute Despotism, it is their right, it is their duty, to throw off such Government, and to provide new Guards for their future security. --Such has been the patient sufferance of these Colonies; and such is now the necessity which constrains them to alter their former Systems of Government.

The history of the present King of Great Britain is a history of repeated injuries and usurpations, all having in direct object the establishment of an absolute Tyranny over these States. To prove this, let Facts be submitted to a candid world.

He has refused his Assent to Laws, the most wholesome and necessary for the public good.

He has forbidden his Governors to pass Laws of immediate and pressing importance, unless suspended in their operation till his Assent should be obtained; and when so suspended, he has utterly neglected to attend to them.

He has refused to pass other Laws for the accommodation of large districts of people, unless those people would relinquish the right of Representation in the Legislature, a right inestimable to them and formidable to tyrants only.

He has called together legislative bodies at places unusual, uncomfortable, and distant from the depository of their Public Records, for the sole purpose of fatiguing them into compliance with his measures.

He has dissolved Representative Houses repeatedly, for opposing with manly firmness his invasions on the rights of the people.

He has refused for a long time, after such dissolutions, to cause others to be elected; whereby the Legislative Powers, incapable of Annihilation, have returned to the People at large for their exercise; the State remaining in the mean time exposed to all the dangers of invasion from without, and convulsions within.

He has endeavoured to prevent the population of these States; for that purpose obstructing the Laws of Naturalization of Foreigners; refusing to pass others to encourage their migration hither, and raising the conditions of new Appropriations of Lands.

He has obstructed the Administration of Justice, by refusing his Assent to Laws for establishing Judiciary Powers.

He has made judges dependent on his Will alone, for the tenure of their offices, and the amount and payment of their salaries.

He has erected a multitude of New Offices, and sent hither swarms of Officers to harass our People, and eat out their substance.

He has kept among us, in times of peace, Standing Armies without the Consent of our legislatures.

He has affected to render the Military independent of and superior to the Civil Power.

He has combined with others to subject us to a jurisdiction foreign to our constitution, and unacknowledged by our laws; giving his Assent to their Acts of pretended legislation:

For quartering large bodies of armed troops among us:

For protecting them, by a mock Trial, from Punishment for any Murders which they should commit on the Inhabitants of these States:

For cutting off our Trade with all parts of the world:

For imposing taxes on us without our Consent:

For depriving us, in many cases, of the benefits of Trial by Jury:

For transporting us beyond Seas to be tried for pretended offences:

For abolishing the free System of English Laws in a neighbouring Province, establishing therein an Arbitrary government, and enlarging its Boundaries so as to render it at once an example and fit instrument for introducing the same absolute rule into these Colonies:

For taking away our Charters, abolishing our most valuable Laws, and altering fundamentally the Forms of our Governments:

For suspending our own Legislatures, and declaring themselves invested with Power to legislate for us in all cases whatsoever.

He has abdicated Government here, by declaring us out of his Protection and waging War against us.

He has plundered our seas, ravaged our Coasts, burnt our towns, and destroyed the lives of our people.

He is at this time transporting large armies of foreign mercenaries to compleat the works of death, desolation and tyranny, already begun with circumstances of Cruelty & perfidy scarcely paralleled in the most barbarous ages, and totally unworthy of the Head of a civilized nation.

He has constrained our fellow Citizens taken Captive on the high Seas to bear Arms against their Country, to become the executioners of their friends and Brethren, or to fall themselves by their Hands.

He has excited domestic insurrections amongst us, and has endeavoured to bring on the inhabitants of our frontiers, the merciless Indian Savages, whose known rule of warfare, is an undistinguished destruction of all ages, sexes and conditions.

In every stage of these Oppressions We have Petitioned for Redress in the most humble terms: Our repeated Petitions have been answered only by repeated injury. A Prince, whose character is thus marked by every act which may define a Tyrant, is unfit to be the ruler of a free People.

Nor have We been wanting in attention to our British brethren. We have warned them from time to time of attempts by their legislature to extend an unwarrantable jurisdiction over us. We have reminded them of the circumstances of our emigration and settlement here. We have appealed to their native justice and magnanimity, and we have conjured them by the ties of our common kindred to disavow these usurpations, which would inevitably interrupt our connections and correspondence. They too have been deaf to the voice of justice and of consanguinity. We must, therefore, acquiesce in the necessity, which denounces our Separation, and hold them, as we hold the rest of mankind, Enemies in War, in Peace Friends.

We, therefore, the Representatives of the United States of America, in General Congress, Assembled, appealing to the Supreme Judge of the world for the rectitude of our intentions, do, in the Name, and by the Authority of the good People of these Colonies, solemnly publish and declare, That these United Colonies are, and of Right ought to be Free and Independent States; that they are Absolved from all Allegiance to the British Crown, and that all political connection between them and the State of Great Britain, is and ought to be totally dissolved; and that as Free and Independent States, they have full Power to levy War, conclude Peace, contract Alliances, establish Commerce, and to do all other Acts and Things which Independent States may of right do. And for the support of this Declaration, with a firm reliance on the Protection of Divine Providence, we mutually pledge to each other our Lives, our Fortunes and our sacred Honor.

TIPS FOR THE TRAIL

Survival - Bear Tracks

America
by Samuel Francis Smith

My country 'tis of thee
Sweet land of liberty:
Of thee I sing.
Land where my fathers died
Land of the Pilgrims' pride
From every mountainside
Let freedom ring.

My native country—thee
Land of the noble free
Thy name I love:
I love thy rocks and rills
Thy woods and templed hills
My heart with rapture thrills
Like that above.

Let music swell the breeze
And ring from all the trees
Sweet freedom's song.
Let all that breathe partake
Let mortal tongues awake
Let rocks their silence break
The sound prolong.

Our fathers' God to thee
Author of liberty
To thee we sing.
Long may our land be bright
With freedom's holy light
Protect us by thy might
Great God, our King.

TIPS FOR THE TRAIL

Navigation - Direction From a Crescent Moon

You can draw a line between the two horns of a crescent moon, whether waning or waxing. The point where this line intersects the horizon will be approximately South. And remember that the moon rises approximately in the East and sets approximately in the West.

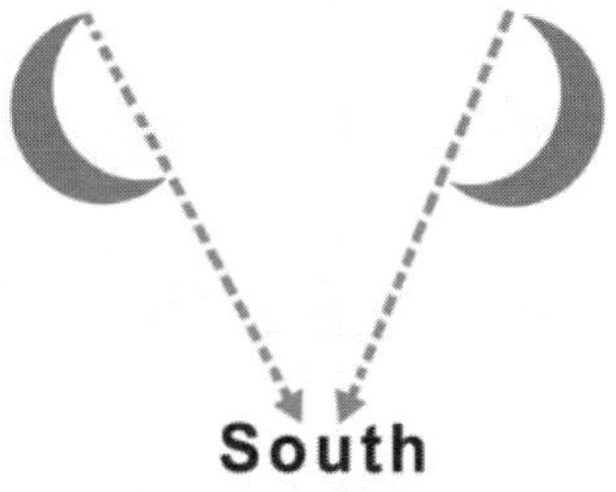

America, The Beautiful
by Katharine Lee Bates

O beautiful for spacious skies,
For amber waves of grain,
For purple mountain majesties
Above the fruited plain!!
America! America!
God shed His grace on thee
And crown thy good with brotherhood
From sea to shining sea!

O beautiful for pilgrim feet,
Whose stern, impassioned stress
A thoroughfare for freedom beat
Across the wilderness!
America! America!
God mend thine every flaw,
Confirm thy soul in self control,
Thy liberty in law!

O beautiful for heroes proved
In liberating strife,
Who more than self their country loved,
And mercy more than life!
America! America!
May God thy gold refine,
Till all success be nobleness
And every gain divine!

O beautiful for patriot dream
That sees beyond the years
Thine alabaster cities gleam
Undimmed by human tears!
America! America!
God shed His grace on thee,
And crown thy good with brotherhood
From sea to shining sea!

TIPS FOR THE TRAIL

What to Do...If Attacked by a Mountain Lion

- Don't hike alone. Keep your kids/dogs close by.
- Never run away--NEVER!
- Make yourself look as big as possible. Open your coat, stand tall. Never crouch or stoop down.
- Slowly back away but never turn your back.
- If attacked, fight back as hard as possible. Do not play dead or roll into a ball.

Paul Revere's Ride
by Henry Wadsworth Longfellow

Listen, my children, and you shall hear
Of the midnight ride of Paul Revere,
On the eighteenth of April, in Seventy-five;
Hardly a man is now alive
Who remembers that famous day and year.

He said to his friend, "If the British march
By land or sea from the town to-night,
Hang a lantern aloft in the belfry arch
Of the North Church tower as a signal light,—
One if by land, and two if by sea;
And I on the opposite shore will be,
Ready to ride and spread the alarm
Through every Middlesex village and farm,
For the country folk to be up and to arm."

Then he said "Good-night!" and with muffled oar
Silently rowed to the Charlestown shore,
Just as the moon rose over the bay,
Where swinging wide at her moorings lay
The Somerset, British man-of-war;
A phantom ship, with each mast and spar
Across the moon like a prison bar,
And a huge black hulk, that was magnified
By its own reflection in the tide.

Meanwhile, his friend through alley and street
Wanders and watches, with eager ears,
Till in the silence around him he hears
The muster of men at the barrack door,
The sound of arms, and the tramp of feet,
And the measured tread of the grenadiers,
Marching down to their boats on the shore.

Then he climbed the tower of the Old North Church,
By the wooden stairs, with stealthy tread,
To the belfry chamber overhead,
And startled the pigeons from their perch
On the sombre rafters, that round him made
Masses and moving shapes of shade,—
By the trembling ladder, steep and tall,
To the highest window in the wall,
Where he paused to listen and look down
A moment on the roofs of the town
And the moonlight flowing over all.

Beneath, in the churchyard, lay the dead,
In their night encampment on the hill,
Wrapped in silence so deep and still
That he could hear, like a sentinel's tread,
The watchful night-wind, as it went
Creeping along from tent to tent,
And seeming to whisper, "All is well!"
A moment only he feels the spell,
Of the place and the hour, and the secret dread
Of the lonely belfry and the dead;
For suddenly all his thoughts are bent
On a shadowy something far away,
Where the river widens to meet the bay,—
A line of black that bends and floats
On the rising tide like a bridge of boats.

Meanwhile, impatient to mount and ride,
Booted and spurred, with a heavy stride
On the opposite shore walked Paul Revere.
Now he patted his horse's side,
Now he gazed at the landscape far and near,
Then, impetuous, stamped the earth,
And turned and tightened his saddle girth;
But mostly he watched with eager search—
The belfry tower of the Old North Church,
As it rose above the graves on the hill,
Lonely and spectral and sombre and still.
And lo! as be looks, on the belfry's height
A glimmer, and then a gleam of light!
He springs to the saddle, the bridle he turns,
But lingers and gazes, till full on his sight
A second lamp in the belfry burns.

A hurry of hoofs in a village street,
A shape in the moonlight, a bulk in the dark,
And beneath, from the pebbles, in passing, a spark
Struck out by a steed flying fearless and fleet;
That was all! And yet, through the gloom and the light,
The fate of a nation was riding that night;
And the spark struck out by that steed, in his flight,
Kindled the land into flame with its heat.

He has left the village and mounted the steep,
And beneath him, tranquil and broad and deep,
Is the Mystic, meeting the ocean tides;
And under the alders that skirt its edge,
Now soft on the sand, now loud on the ledge,
Is heard the tramp of his steed as he rides.

It was twelve by the village clock
When he crossed the bridge into Medford town.
He heard the crowing of the cock,
And the barking of the farmer's dog,
And felt the damp of the river fog,
That rises after the sun goes down.
It was one by the village clock,
When he galloped into Lexington.
He saw the gilded weathercock
Swim in the moonlight as he passed,
And the meeting-house windows, black and bare,
Gaze at him with a spectral glare,
As if they already stood aghast
At the bloody work they would look upon.

It was two by the village clock,
When he came to the bridge in Concord town.
He heard the bleating of the flock,
And the twitter of birds among the trees,
And felt the breath of the morning breeze
Blowing over the meadow brown.
And one was safe and asleep in his bed
Who at the bridge would be first to fall,
Who that day would be lying dead,
Pierced by a British musket ball.

You know the rest. In the books you have read
How the British Regulars fired and fled,—
How the farmers gave them ball for ball,
From behind each fence and farmyard wall,
Chasing the redcoats down the lane,
Then crossing the fields to emerge again
Under the trees at the turn of the road,
And only pausing to fire and load.

So through the night rode Paul Revere;
And so through the night went his cry of alarm
To every Middlesex village and farm,—
A cry of defiance, and not of fear,
A voice in the darkness, a knock at the door,
And a word that shall echo for evermore!
For, borne on the night-wind of the Past,
Through all our history, to the last,
In the hour of darkness and peril and need,
The people will waken and listen to hear
The hurrying hoof-beats of that steed,
And the midnight message of Paul Revere.

Concord Hymn
by Ralph Waldo Emerson

By the rude bridge that arched the flood,
Their flag to April's breeze unfurled,
Here once the embattled farmers stood,
And fired the shot heard round the world.

The foe long since in silence slept;
Alike the conqueror silent sleeps;
And Time the ruined bridge has swept
Down the dark stream which seaward creeps.

On this green bank, by this soft stream,
We set today a votive stone;
That memory may their deed redeem,
When, like our sires, our sons are gone.

Spirit, that made those spirits dare
To die, and leave their children free,
Bid Time and Nature gently spare
The shaft we raise to them and thee.

The Charge of the Light Brigade
by Alfred Lord Tennyson

This poems honors a suicidal charge by the British against Russian cannons in the Crimean War of 1853-1856.

Half a league, half a league,
Half a league onward,
All in the valley of Death
Rode the six hundred.
"Forward, the Light Brigade!
Charge for the guns!" he said—.
Into the valley of Death
Rode the six hundred.

"Forward, the Light Brigade!"
Was there a man dismayed?
Not tho' the soldiers knew
Some one had blundered:
Theirs not to make reply,
Theirs not to reason why,
Theirs but to do and die.
Into the valley of Death
Rode the six hundred.

Cannon to right of them,
Cannon to left of them,
Cannon in front of them
    Volleyed and thunder'd;
Storm'd at with shot and shell,
Boldly they rode and well,
Into the jaws of Death,
Into the mouth of Hell,
    Rode the six hundred.

Flashed all their sabres bare,
Flashed as they turned in air,
Sab'ring the gunners there,
Charging an army, while
    All the world wondered:
Plunged in the battery smoke,
Right through the line they broke;
Cossack and Russian
Reeled from the sabre-stroke
    Shattered and sundered.
Then they rode back, but not—
    Not the six hundred.

Cannon to right of them,
Cannon to left of them
Cannon behind them
    Volleyed and thundered;
Stormed at with shot and shell,
While horse and hero fell,
They that had fought so well
Came thro' the jaws of Death,
Back from the mouth of Hell,
All that was left of them,
    Left of six hundred.

When can their glory fade?
Oh, the wild charge they made!
    All the world wondered.
Honor the charge they made!
Honor the Light Brigade,
    Noble Six Hundred!

The Gettysburg Address
by Abraham Lincoln

This speech at the Dedication of the National Cemetery at Gettysburg, Pennsylvania, November 19, 1863, took Abraham Lincoln just 2 minutes to deliver. His fellow speaker, Edward Everett, took 2 hours to deliver a speech no one remembers.

Fourscore and seven years ago our fathers brought forth upon this continent a new nation, conceived in liberty, and dedicated to the proposition that all men are created equal. Now we are engaged in a great civil war, testing whether that nation, or any nation so conceived and so dedicated, can long endure. We are met on a great battlefield of that war. We have come to dedicate a portion of that field as a final resting-place for those who here gave their lives that that nation might live. It is altogether fitting and proper that we should do this. But in a larger sense we cannot dedicate, we cannot consecrate, we cannot hallow this ground. The brave men, living and dead, who struggled here, have consecrated it far above our poor power to add or detract. The world will little note, nor long remember, what we say here; but it can never forget what they did here. It is for us, the living, rather to be dedicated here to the unfinished work which they who fought here have thus far so nobly advanced. It is rather for us to be here dedicated to the great task remaining before us, that from these honored dead we take increased devotion to that cause for which they gave the last full measure of devotion; that we here highly resolve that these dead shall not have died in vain; that this nation, under God, shall have a new birth of freedom, and that government of the people, by the people, and for the people, shall not perish from the earth.

TIPS FOR THE TRAIL

Navigation - Convert Magnetic to True Bearing

Maps are usually oriented to true north. A compass gives you readings based on magnetic north, which can differ from True North by more than 20°. To convert your bearings, refer to the following chart. Your maps will show you the value of your local declination, either on the compass rose or in the legend somewhere.

Compass°	+ East Declination°	= True°
Compass°	- West Declination°	= True°
True°	- East Declination°	= Compass°
True°	+ West Declination°	= Compass°

The Spell of the Yukon
by Robert Service

I wanted the gold, and I sought it;
    I scrabbled and mucked like a slave.
Was it famine or scurvy—I fought it;
    I hurled my youth into a grave.
I wanted the gold, and I got it—
    Came out with a fortune last fall,—
Yet somehow life's not what I thought it,
    And somehow the gold isn't all.

No! There's the land. (Have you seen it?)
    It's the cussedest land that I know,
From the big, dizzy mountains that screen it
    To the deep, deathlike valleys below.
Some say God was tired when He made it;
    Some say it's a fine land to shun;
Maybe; but there's some as would trade it
    For no land on earth—and I'm one.

You come to get rich (damned good reason);
    You feel like an exile at first;
You hate it like hell for a season,
    And then you are worse than the worst.
It grips you like some kinds of sinning;
    It twists you from foe to a friend;
It seems it's been since the beginning;
    It seems it will be to the end.

I've stood in some mighty-mouthed hollow
    That's plumb-full of hush to the brim;
I've watched the big, husky sun wallow
    In crimson and gold, and grow dim,
Till the moon set the pearly peaks gleaming,
    And the stars tumbled out, neck and crop;
And I've thought that I surely was dreaming,
    With the peace o' the world piled on top.

The summer—no sweeter was ever;
    The sunshiny woods all athrill;
The grayling aleap in the river,
    The bighorn asleep on the hill.
The strong life that never knows harness;
    The wilds where the caribou call;
The freshness, the freedom, the fairness—
    O God! how I'm stuck on it all.

The winter! the brightness that blinds you,
The white land locked tight as a drum,
The cold fear that follows and finds you,
The silence that bludgeons you dumb.
The snows that are older than history,
The woods where the weird shadows slant;
The stillness, the moonlight, the mystery,
I've bade 'em good-by—but I can't.

There's a land where the mountains are nameless,
And the rivers all run God knows where;
There are lives that are erring and aimless,
And deaths that just hang by a hair;
There are hardships that nobody reckons;
There are valleys unpeopled and still;
There's a land—oh, it beckons and beckons,
And I want to go back—and I will.

They're making my money diminish;
I'm sick of the taste of champagne.
Thank God! when I'm skinned to a finish
I'll pike to the Yukon again.
I'll fight—and you bet it's no sham-fight;
It's hell!—but I've been there before;
And it's better than this by a damsite—
So me for the Yukon once more.

There's gold, and it's haunting and haunting;
It's luring me on as of old;
Yet it isn't the gold that I'm wanting
So much as just finding the gold.
It's the great, big, broad land 'way up yonder,
It's the forests where silence has lease;
It's the beauty that thrills me with wonder,
It's the stillness that fills me with peace.

TIPS FOR THE TRAIL

Navigation - Determining Distance of Objects

6 miles = You can recognize large houses and towers.
2 miles = Vehicles seen moving, windows seen as dots.
1 mile = People look like dots, tree trunks can be seen.
1/2 mile = Branches of trees are visible.
1/4 mile = Clothing color is visible; leg movement seen.
250 yds = Faces are blurs.
100 yds = Eyes can be seen as dots.
50 yds = You can see eyes and mouth clearly.

Sometimes
by Thomas S. Jones, Jr.

Across the fields of yesterday
He sometimes comes to me,
A little lad just back from play—
The lad I used to be.

And yet he smiles so wistfully
Once he has crept within,
I wonder if he hopes to see
The man I might have been.

A Bag of Tools
by R. L. Sharpe

Isn't it strange
That princes and kings,
And clowns that caper
In sawdust rings,
And common people
Like you and me
Are builders for eternity?

Each is given a bag of tools,
A shapeless mass,
A book of rules;
And each must make—
Ere life is flown—
A stumbling block
Or a steppingstone.

TIPS FOR THE TRAIL

Cooking - At High Altitudes

- At sea level, water boils at 212°F
- At 5000 ft, water boils at around 200°F
- At 10,000 ft, water boils at around 194°F
- Add more water to recipes.
- If boiling food, boil for a longer time. If baking, increase the temperature of the oven. You can usually use less baking soda and powder.
- Soak dehydrated foods longer.
- Read the recipes on the food container. They will usually give directions for high altitude cooking.

Because I Could Not Stop For Death
by Emily Dickinson

Because I could not stop for Death,
He kindly stopped for me;
The carriage held but just ourselves,
And Immortality.

We slowly drove, he knew no haste,
And I had put away
My labor, and my leisure too,
For his civility.

We passed the school where children played,
Their lessons scarcely done;
We passed the fields of grazing grain,
We passed the setting sun.

We paused before a house that seemed
A swelling of the ground;
The roof was scarcely visible,
The cornice but a mound.

Since then 'tis centuries; but each
Feels shorter than the day
I first surmised the horses' heads
Were toward eternity.

TIPS FOR THE TRAIL

Knots - Bowline

You need to be able to tie this in the dark. Useful for loops for rescuing people; doesn't jam. Make a loop in the long line with the long line on the bottom. Then, as the saying goes, go up the hole with the loose end, around the tree and back down the hole again.

Knots - Square Knot

A general knot for tying two lines together. However, it is not a completely secure knot so you should use other knots like the bowline where required.

The Road Not Taken
by Robert Frost

Two roads diverged in a yellow wood,
And sorry I could not travel both
And be one traveler, long I stood
And looked down one as far as I could
To where it bent in the undergrowth;

Then took the other, as just as fair,
And having perhaps the better claim,
Because it was grassy and wanted wear;
Though as for that the passing there
Had worn them really about the same,

And both that morning equally lay
In leaves no step had trodden black.
Oh, I kept the first for another day!
Yet knowing how way leads on to way,
I doubted if I should ever come back.

I shall be telling this with a sigh
Somewhere ages and ages hence:
Two roads diverged in a wood, and I--
I took the one less traveled by,
And that has made all the difference.

TIPS FOR THE TRAIL

First Aid - Choking (Heimlich maneuver)

1. First, make sure that the victim is indeed choking. Encourage coughing as that may free the airway.
2. Ask the victim if he is choking. If he can't answer or nods his head, you will need to take action.
3. Stand behind the victim. Place your arms around his waist and clamp them together with the knuckle of one thumb pressing inward above the navel and below the rib cage.
4. Pull both hands toward you quickly with an upward and inward thrust. You want to force air out of the lungs to dislodge the obstruction.
5. Repeat until the airway is clear.

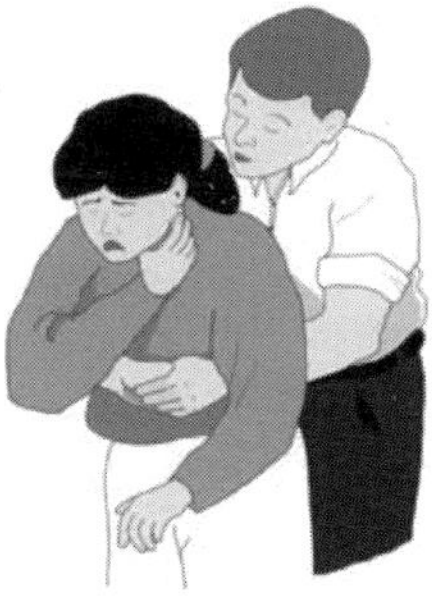

The Arrow and the Song
by Henry Wadsworth Longfellow

I shot an arrow into the air,
It fell to earth, I knew not where;
For, so swiftly it flew, the sight
Could not follow it in its flight.

I breathed a song into the air,
It fell to earth, I knew not where;
For who has sight so keen and strong,
That it can follow the flight of song?

Long, long afterward, in an oak
I found the arrow, still unbroke;
And the song, from beginning to end,
I found again in the heart of a friend.

TIPS FOR THE TRAIL

Cooking - Treating Water

Besides bad odor and taste, water from questionable sources may be contaminated by Giardia and other organisms that cause disease. If you have the slightest doubt, purify before use--don't take a chance. Strain water before treating to remove suspended material. Avoid water that may have toxic chemicals, or contains dead animals.

Water Pump

You need a pump with pores smaller than 1 micron to filter Giardia and Cryptosporidium, and 0.2 micron pores to get rid of all bacteria, while iodinated resin will help remove viruses. Follow directions that come with the pump. Be sure to clean the pump at recommended intervals.

Boil

Bring the water to a boil. As soon as it boils, the water should be safe to drink as most organisms, including Giardia, are destroyed at temperatures below boiling, even at higher altitudes where the boiling point is lower. To be fully safe (and if you have enough fuel), keep the water at a rolling boil for one minute. Afterwards, pour the water back and forth between containers to improve the taste.

Iodine tablets

Follow the iodine tablet package directions. It takes longer to disinfect colder water. You will normally need to wait 15 minutes for warm water and up to 45 minutes for cold water to disinfect. Also, cloudy water will need either more tablets or more time to disinfect properly. Iodine will **not** kill Cryptosporidium so be careful.

I Died For Beauty
by Emily Dickinson.

I died for beauty but was scarce
Adjusted in the tomb,
When one who died for truth was lain
In an adjoining room.

He questioned softly why I failed?
"For beauty," I replied.
"And I for truth, the two are one;
We brethren are," he said.

And so, as kinsmen met a night,
We talked between the rooms,
Until the moss had reached our lips,
And covered up our names.

TIPS FOR THE TRAIL

First Aid - Blisters
Blisters form when friction separates the inner and outer layer of skin, which dies after the area fills with fluid.

Avoiding Blisters
- BREAK IN YOUR BOOTS BEFORE YOUR HIKE!
- Wear sock liners--thin socks that go under your regular thick wool socks and absorb sweat and reduce friction.
- Keep your socks and feet dry. When you stop, remove your boots and socks, cool your feet in water, dry them and put dry socks on.

Catching Hotspots Early
- Hot spots are areas that look like they will turn into a blister. Protect the hotspot, then cover the area to prevent further friction. Use tape (even duct tape), moleskin or a 2nd-skin type blister bandage.
- Examine your socks and boots to see if you can eliminate the source of the hotspot.

Treating blisters
1. Clean and dry the skin around the blister.
2. Cut a doughnut shaped piece of moleskin with the hole sized to the blister.
3. Place the moleskin over the blister and smooth it out. This prevents further pressure and friction.
4. Don't pop the blister unless you think it will pop as you walk. To pop it, clean the area with soap and water. Sterilize a needle with a match, puncture around the sides, and drain the fluid. Apply antibiotic ointment and a clean, dry bandage. Check and clean each night.

Jabberwocky

by Lewis Carroll from *Through the Looking-Glass*

As explained to Alice, these fantasy words mean: *brillig*=4pm before dinner when you start broiling things; *slithy*=lithe and slimy; *toves*=a combo badger/lizard/corkscrew; *gyre*=go round like a gyroscope; *gimble*=make holes like a gimlet; *wabe*=grass plot around a sun-dial; *mimsy*=flimsy and miserable; *borogove*=thin shabby looking bird; *mome raths*=green pigs away from home; o*utgrabe*=something between bellowing and whistling with a sneeze in between.

`Twas brillig, and the slithy toves
Did gyre and gimble in the wabe:
All mimsy were the borogoves,
And the mome raths outgrabe.

"Beware the Jabberwock, my son!
The jaws that bite, the claws that catch!
Beware the Jubjub bird, and shun
The frumious Bandersnatch!"

He took his vorpal sword in hand:
Long time the manxome foe he sought --
So rested he by the Tumtum tree,
And stood awhile in thought.

And, as in uffish thought he stood,
The Jabberwock, with eyes of flame,
Came whiffling through the tulgey wood,
And burbled as it came!

One, two! One, two! And through and through
The vorpal blade went snicker-snack!
He left it dead, and with its head
He went galumphing back.

"And, has thou slain the Jabberwock?
Come to my arms, my beamish boy!
O frabjous day! Callooh! Callay!"
He chortled in his joy.

`Twas brillig, and the slithy toves
Did gyre and gimble in the wabe;
All mimsy were the borogoves,
And the mome raths outgrabe.

TIPS FOR THE TRAIL

Knots - Timber Hitch

Used to attach ropes to logs so that you can drag them. It is tight under strain, but will loosen when tension is removed.

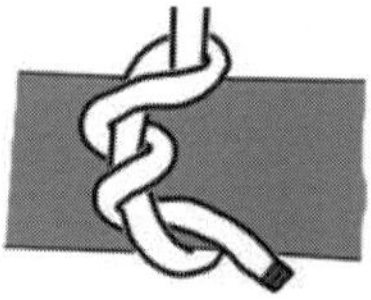

This Land is Your Land
by Woody Guthrie

This land is your land
This land is my land
From California to the New York island
From the redwood forests to the Gulf Stream waters
This land was made for you and me.

As I was walking that ribbon of highway,
I saw above me that endless skyway;
I saw below me that golden valley;
This land was made for you and me.

I've roamed and rambled and I followed my footsteps
To the sparkling sands of her diamond deserts;
And all around me a voice was sounding;
This land was made for you and me.

When the sun came shining, and I was strolling,
And the wheat fields waving and the dust clouds rolling,
As the fog was lifting a voice was chanting;
This land was made for you and me.

As I went walking, I saw a sign there,
And on the sign it said "No Trespassing."
But on the other side it didn't say nothing,
That side was made for you and me.

In the shadow of the steeple I saw my people,
By the relief office I seen my people;
As they stood there hungry, I stood there asking
Is this land made for you and me?

Nobody living can ever stop me,
As I go walking that freedom highway;
Nobody living can ever make me turn back,
This land was made for you and me.

TIPS FOR THE TRAIL

First Aid - Shock

Shock normally accompanies major injuries and trauma. The victim can be weak, clammy, pale with a weak pulse and rapid breathing. You should normally treat the victim of any injury for shock as this may help prevent it.

1. Treat the injury or trauma that caused the shock.
2. Ensure that the victim's airway is open.
3. Lie the victim down with the feet raised.
4. Keep the victim warm. Cover with a blanket.
5. Stay calm and keep the victim calm. Talk calmly.

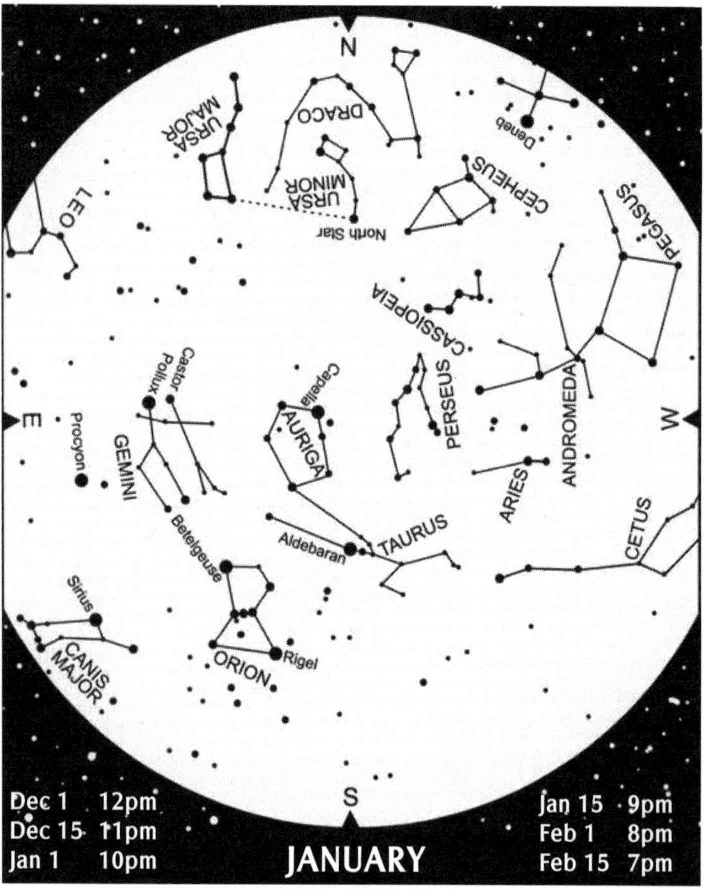

STAR CHARTS

1. Find the star map that has the date (in lower corners) closest to your current date and note the associated time.
2. Next, adjust for your current time. Move one map forward (e.g. Jan to Apr) for every 6 hours later in time, or one map backward (e.g. Oct to Jul) for every 6 hours earlier in time it is from the printed time found in step 1.
3. Example: To find the stars for 6 am on Dec 1, first find a map with Dec 1 listed. You find it on the January map and note that it indicates "12pm". Add 6 hours (12pm to your 6am) which moves you one map forward to the April map. You may end up in between, with stars from two maps. Stars and planets move 15 degrees CCW around the North Star each hour.
4. To use the map, hold it over your head with the top (N) facing toward the North. Or, turn the map until the direction at the bottom matches the direction you are facing. These charts work for mid Northern Latitudes--you may see different stars.

Many cultures had stories or myths about the stars and constellations they saw in their sky. We have included stories mostly from Greek mythology that they used to explain the heavens.

January Stars

Cepheus, Cassiopeia, Perseus, Andromeda, Cetus, Pegasus

Cassiopeia was an Ethiopian queen who was so vain that she boasted she and her daughter **Andromeda** were prettier than the sea nymphs. Poseidon, the sea god, sent a horrible sea monster, **Cetus** (now known as the Whale), to punish her country. **Cetus** was soon laying waste to her land and killing her people. Her husband **Cepheus**, the King, was told by an oracle that he had to offer his lovely daughter **Andromeda** as a sacrifice to be eaten by the monster. She was soon chained to the rocks by the ocean, awaiting certain death. The monster **Cetus** was soon approaching the rocks where she lay chained. However, the brave warrior, **Perseus**, after slaying the hideous creature Medusa, came across **Andromeda** and killed the monster, claiming **Andromeda** as his bride. Some of the blood from Medusa's severed head fell into the sea and was used by Poseidon to make the Winged Horse, **Pegasus**.

Orion, Taurus, Canis Major, Auriga

Orion is the Great Hunter and one of the most recognizable constellations in the sky. He faces us with the top stars representing his shoulders, the three horizontal stars his belt, and the three close vertical stars his sword. The two lower stars are his feet. The right star of his belt is special since it rises due East and sets due West. **Orion** is looking up to his side at **Taurus**, the Bull. Aldebaran, the bright star in **Taurus**, is the bull's right eye. The bull's head is lowered and the tips of his horns are above **Orion**. You see only the top part of **Taurus** since this represents the bull into which Jupiter changed himself while swimming to Crete carrying the princess Europa. Only the top half of the bull was visible above the water. You can also see the largest of **Orion**'s hunting dogs, **Canis Major**, at his feet waiting to help. Its bright star, Sirius, is also known as the Dog Star. Capella is the star directly overhead in the constellation **Auriga**, the Charioteer. **Auriga** helped **Orion** after **Orion** had been blinded.

Gemini

The constellation **Gemini** represents the twin sons of Leda and Zeus, Castor and Pollux, which are the names of the bright stars at their heads. They were the half brothers of Helen of Troy. Castor was killed and Pollux begged Zeus that they not be separated, so Zeus placed them both in the sky together.

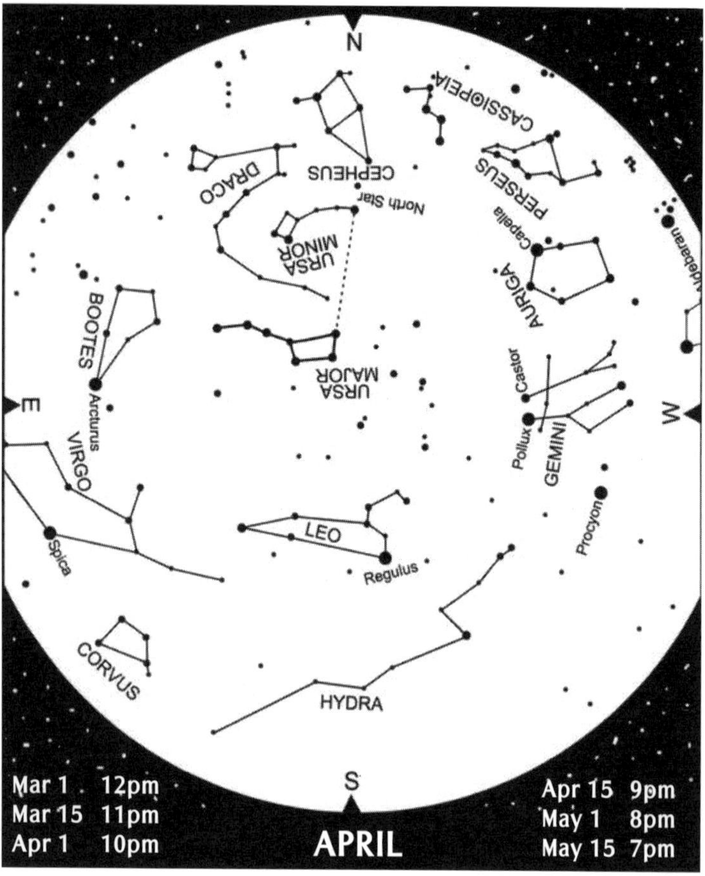

April Stars

Hydra, Corvus

Hydra, the Water Serpent, is the longest constellation in the sky, stretching across the southern sky. Close to its tail is the Raven, **Corvus**. One story is that the Sun-god, Apollo, sent his pet raven down to Earth to bring him back some water. At the spring, the raven saw a fig tree with ripening fruit. The bird decided to wait until the fruit ripened, and then waited longer to eat the ripened fruit. He was finally ready to return to Apollo with his water, but knew the god would be angry at the delay. So, he captured a water serpent, **Hydra**, on his way back. He explained that the serpent had attacked him, causing the delay. Apollo was not so easily tricked and, enraged, he threw **Corvus** and the serpent into the sky.

Leo

Leo, the Lion, stands facing to the right in the southern sky. The bright star, Regulus, is below his head. **Hercules** (see next map) had to kill the Nemean lion for his first labor. The lion's hide was so tough that no weapons could pierce it. Hercules finally strangled the lion to death and returned with his body. He later skinned the lion and used his hide as a protective shield. Hera, the goddess, became so angry at **Hercules** that she placed the lion into the sky as the constellation **Leo**.

Ursa Major, Ursa Minor, Bootes

The god Zeus fell in love with a beautiful maiden named Callisto. Unfortunately, Zeus's wife, Hera, found out and punished the girl by turning her into a bear. One day she was approached by a hunter whom she suddenly recognized to be her son Arcas. As she ran forward to embrace him, he readied his spear to stop the bear. Zeus changed Arcas into a bear to prevent the killing. He then swung them both by their tails and placed them in the sky as **Ursa Major** and **Ursa Minor**. Hera then forbade them to enter the seas so they constantly circle the North Star and never set. The handle of each dipper represents the tail of the bear. The constellation **Bootes** is called the Bear Driver and controls the Hunting Dogs and seems to continuously chase the bears around the sky.

Draco

Long ago, the younger gods entered a 10-year battle with the older gods, pitting gods like Athena and Zeus against the giant Titans of Earth. A Titan hurled a huge dragon at Athena who deftly caught the dragon and hurled him into the heavens. This dragon, **Draco,** twisted and coiled and became tied in knots until he finally landed, twisted and asleep, coiled between **Ursa Major** and **Ursa Minor**.

Virgo

Virgo lays low in the eastern sky this time of year. She probably represents the Greek goddess Demeter who was the Earth-goddess. The God of the Underground, Hades, fell in love with her daughter, Persephone, and wanted to marry her. Her mother did not want this to happen. Hades carried her off in his chariot to the Underworld. When she did not return home, Demeter went to look for her. Hades was told he must let Persephone leave with her mother but by then, Persephone had fallen in love with Hades. Zeus resolved the crisis by having Persephone spend half of her time with Hades and half with her mother. Every winter, Persephone leaves Earth to go to the Underworld, and every Spring she returns to Olympus, bringing warmth and light back to Earth.

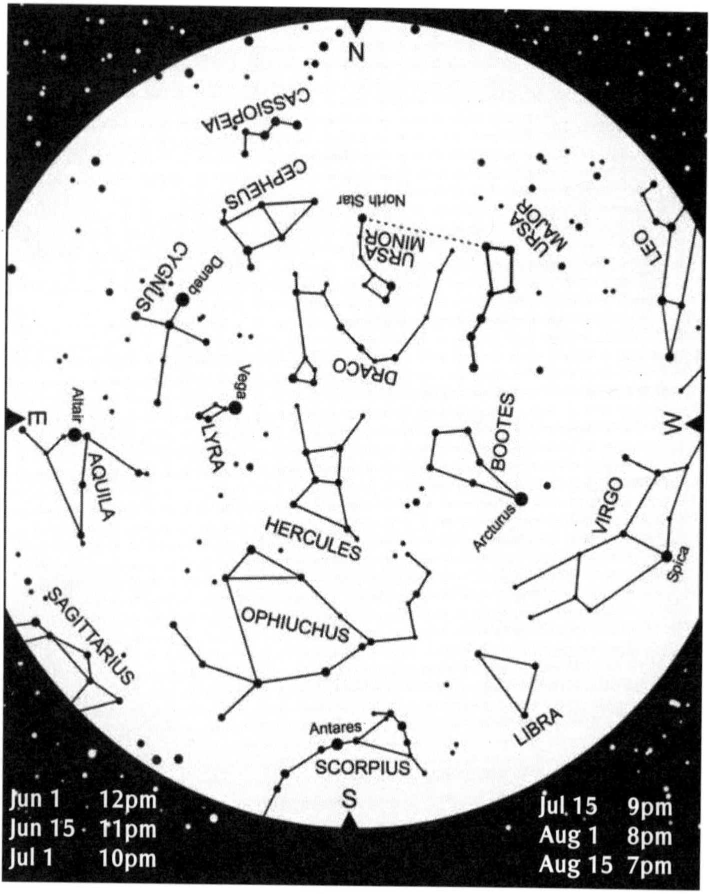

July Stars

Sagittarius, Scorpius

Sagittarius, the Archer, is low in the SE sky to the left of **Scorpius**. According to one myth, **Sagittarius** is shown ready to shoot an arrow through **Scorpius** if he threatens anyone. **Sagittarius** is normally represented as a centaur, half man and half horse. He most likely is Chiron, a friend of Hercules who was accidently killed by one of his arrows.

Orion, Scorpius

Another myth linked **Orion** (see January map) and **Scorpius**. The Goddess of Earth, Gaea, was concerned about **Orion**'s boasts that he could kill all the animals on Earth. She decided he must be killed and sent a huge scorpion to string **Orion**. After a brief fight, **Orion** was stung in the heel, represented by the star Rigel, and died. **Orion** and **Scorpius** were both memorialized in the sky, but were placed at opposite sides of the sky so they would never fight again.

Lyra

Vega is the bright star in **Lyra**, the Lyre of Orpheus, which should be almost directly overhead. Orpheus was married to the beautiful Eurydice but she soon died after being bitten by a serpent. Orpheus went to Hades to rescue her, playing his wonderful lyre. Pluto, God of the Underworld, was so enthralled that he agreed to return Eurydice to Earth, on the sole condition that Orpheus not look back at her until they were back in the light. Orpheus agreed, but at the last moment turned to look back and Pluto claimed his bride forever. Sad and forlorn, Orpheus wandered the rest of his life playing his lyre. Chased by beautiful maidens, he refused to wed. The spurned maidens tore his body apart. Zeus, who had also been captivated by Orpheus' music, made his **Lyra** immortal in the sky.

Libra

Libra, the Balance or Scales of Justice, sits low in the sky to the left of **Virgo**. This constellation was not recognized by the Greeks but was identified by the Romans. It was first associated with Julius Caesar and then later with **Virgo**, the Goddess of Justice. A scale was chosen because at the time of its naming, the sun was in this constellation on September 21, the Automnal Equinox. On that day, the day and night are of equal length.

Ophiuchus

Ophiuchus is known as the Serpent-Holder. The main part of this constellation represents **Ophiuchus**, while the serpent trails off to either side, being held in his arms. **Ophiuchus** is a word coming from two Greek words meaning "serpent" and "holding."

Aquila

Aquila, the Eagle, flies across the Eastern sky. During the 10-year battle between the Olympian gods and the giant Titans, **Aquila** helped Zeus by delivering Zeus' thunderbolts to Earth to kill the terrible Titans. He was rewarded by being placed in the sky.

Hercules

After completing the supposedly impossible 12 Labors, the mighty **Hercules** died when his second wife accidentally put poison on his robe. She thought that she was pouring on a magic potion that would make **Hercules** love her again. Instead, it was an awful poison that burned his skin and killed him. Zeus honored his son by making him a god and placing him in the sky forever.

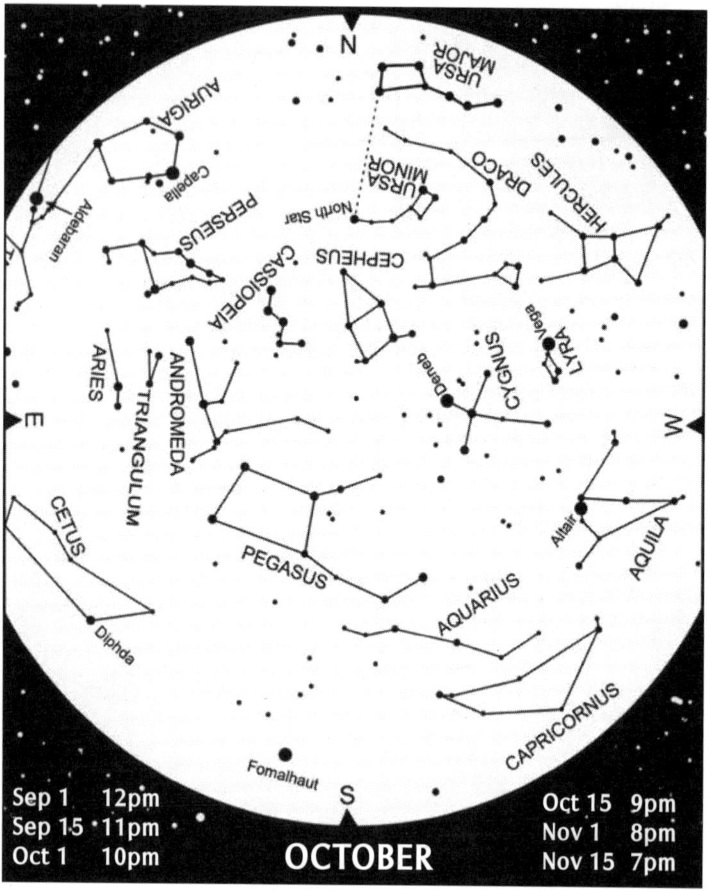

October Stars

Cygnus

Cygnus, the Swan, is also known as the Northern Cross. Phaëthon demanded of his father, the son-god Helios, that he be allowed to drive his mighty sun-chariot for one day. Helios explained how dangerous the chariot was, but could not dissuade his son. Phaëthon started the day's journey smoothly, but soon lost control of the horses as they realized his father was not at the reins. The chariot was soon plunging wildly about. Every time it went too low, fires started and deserts were created. When it went too high, the Earth became very cold. Jupiter finally had enough and struck him down with a thunderbolt. Phaëthon plunged into a river. His friend, Cyenus, tried in vain to find his body. The gods pitied Cyenus and changed him into a swan with his neck constantly in the water looking for his friend. He was transported into the heavens as **Cygnus** the Swan.

Aquarius

Aquarius, the Water-Carrier, lies below **Pegasus**. **Aquarius** caused a great flood in 1500 B.C. which destroyed all life except for Deucalion and Pyrrha, who built a big boat and survived on the waters until the flood waters receded. When they finally landed on dry ground, an oracle advised them to throw rocks over their shoulders. When they did, they discovered the stones had become men and women. Thus, Aquarius is known as both a taker of life and a giver of life. The world flood myth is common among many cultures.

Aries

Aries, the Ram, is known for his golden fleece. Queen Nephele was worried that her husband, King Athamas, would harm her two children, Helle and Phrixus. Mercury helped her by giving her a marvelous golden ram, **Aries**. The two children climbed onto the ram's back and **Aries** flew through the air with the children. Unfortunately, Helle could not hold on and fell into the sea by Turkey, which resulted in those straits being called the Hellespont. Phrixus held on and was carried to safety. The ram was later sacrificed and his golden fleece later rescued by Jason and the Argonauts.

Capricornus

Capricornus, the Sea-Goat, is represented as half-goat and half-fish. The god Typhoon had battled Zeus and defeated him. He cut out the tendons in Zeus' feet and hands and hid them in a cave. The dragon woman Delphyne was chosen to guard the tendons. However, the god Aegipan was able to steal the items and was attempting to escape. Many gods often turned themselves into animals to avoid detection and Aegipan was ready to use this trick as well. He jumped into a river and was partially submerged when he finally decided to be a goat. However, since he was halfway underwater, he became a goat from the waist up only, and a fish from the waist down. He returned the stolen tendons to Zeus who regained his strength. After Zeus killed Typhoon, he honored Aegipan by placing him in the sky as the constellation **Capricornus**.

Triangulum

Triangulum represents the Triangle. It is an older constellation. Zeus wanted to honor the island Sicily and placed **Triangulum** in the sky in its honor.

TIPS FOR THE TRAIL

Knots - Figure Eight

Use at the end of ropes. Will not jam like an overhand knot. Use this in most cases you would use an overhand knot.

Knots - Fisherman's Knot

Useful for combining two ropes of equal size. Fishermen use it to join fishing lines together.

Knots - Sheepshank

Useful to quickly shorten a longer rope. Will not hold consistently, especially if pressure is removed. You can tie another hitch on each end to make slightly more secure.

Knots - SheetBend

Very useful when combining ropes of different diameters. The lighter colored rope is the smaller one.

Knots - Tautline Hitch

A knot you will use all the time. It is adjustable--simply release some tension, slide the knot along the longer line, and retension. Used frequently on guy wires for tents.

Knots - Prussik

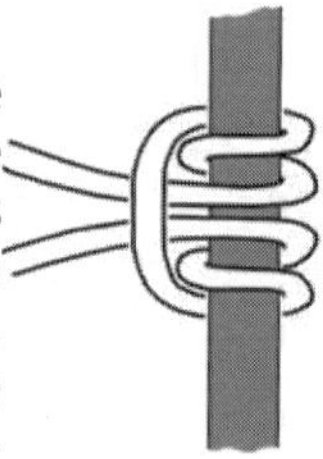

Useful for self-rescue where you have to ascend or descend a rope. The lighter colored rope at the left needs to be a smaller diameter than the main rope. The knot holds under pressure, but can be slid on the larger rope when the pressure is removed. It is often tied in a loop, leaving you a bight into which you can place your foot or hand. With two loops tied on a larger rope, you can climb up or down.

TALES

To Build a Fire
by Jack London

Day had broken cold and grey, exceedingly cold and grey, when the man turned aside from the main Yukon trail and climbed the high earth-bank, where a dim and little-travelled trail led eastward through the fat spruce timberland. It was a steep bank, and he paused for breath at the top, excusing the act to himself by looking at his watch. It was nine o'clock. There was no sun nor hint of sun, though there was not a cloud in the sky. It was a clear day, and yet there seemed an intangible pall over the face of things, a subtle gloom that made the day dark, and that was due to the absence of sun. This fact did not worry the man. He was used to the lack of sun. It had been days since he had seen the sun, and he knew that a few more days must pass before that cheerful orb, due south, would just peep above the sky-line and dip immediately from view.

The man flung a look back along the way he had come. The Yukon lay a mile wide and hidden under three feet of ice. On top of this ice were as many feet of snow. It was all pure white, rolling in gentle undulations where the ice-jams of the freeze-up had formed. North and south, as far as his eye could see, it was unbroken white, save for a dark hair-line that curved and twisted from around the spruce-covered island to the south, and that curved and twisted away into the north, where it disappeared behind another spruce-covered island. This dark hair-line was the trail—the main trail—that led south five hundred miles to the Chilcoot Pass, Dyea, and salt water; and that led north seventy miles to Dawson, and still on to the north a thousand miles to Nulato, and finally to St. Michael on Bering Sea, a thousand miles and half a thousand more.

But all this—the mysterious, far-reaching hairline trail, the absence of sun from the sky, the tremendous cold, and the strangeness and weirdness of it all—made no impression on the man. It was not because he was long used to it. He was a new-comer in the land, a chechaquo, and this was his first winter. The trouble with him was that he was without imagination. He was quick and alert in the things of life, but only in the things, and not in the significances. Fifty degrees below zero meant eighty odd degrees of frost. Such fact impressed him as being cold and uncomfortable, and that was all. It did not lead him to meditate upon his frailty as a creature of temperature, and upon man's frailty in general, able only to live within certain narrow limits of heat and cold; and from there on it did not lead him to the conjectural field of immortality and man's place in the universe. Fifty degrees below zero stood for a bite of frost that hurt and that must be guarded against by the use of mittens, ear-flaps, warm moccasins, and thick socks. Fifty degrees below zero was to him just precisely fifty degrees below zero. That there should be anything more to it than that was a thought that never entered his head.

As he turned to go on, he spat speculatively. There was a sharp, explosive crackle that startled him. He spat again. And again, in the air, before it could fall to the snow, the spittle crackled. He knew that at fifty below spittle crackled on the snow, but this spittle had crackled in the air. Undoubtedly it was colder than fifty below—how much colder he did not know. But the temperature did not matter. He was bound for the old claim on the left fork of Henderson Creek, where the boys were already. They had come over across the divide from the Indian Creek country, while he had come the roundabout way to take a look at the possibilities of getting out logs in the spring from the islands in the Yukon. He would be in to camp by six o'clock; a bit after dark, it was true, but the boys would be there, a fire would be going, and a hot supper would be ready. As for lunch, he pressed his hand against the protruding bundle under his jacket. It was also under his shirt, wrapped up in a handkerchief and lying against the naked skin. It was the only way to keep the biscuits from freezing. He smiled agreeably to himself as he thought of those biscuits, each cut open and sopped in bacon grease, and each enclosing a generous slice of fried bacon.

He plunged in among the big spruce trees. The trail was faint. A foot of snow had fallen since the last sled had passed over, and he was glad he was without a sled, travelling light. In fact, he carried nothing but the lunch wrapped in the handkerchief. He was surprised, however, at the cold. It certainly was cold, he concluded, as he rubbed his numbed nose and cheek-bones with his mittened hand. He was a warm-whiskered man, but the hair on his face did not protect the high cheek-bones and the eager nose that thrust itself aggressively into the frosty air.

At the man's heels trotted a dog, a big native husky, the proper wolf-dog, grey-coated and without any visible or temperamental difference from its brother, the wild wolf. The animal was depressed by the tremendous cold. It knew that it was no time for travelling. Its instinct told it a truer tale than was told to the man by the man's judgment. In reality, it was not merely colder than fifty below zero; it was colder than sixty below, than seventy below. It was seventy-five below zero. Since the freezing-point is thirty-two above zero, it meant that one hundred and seven degrees of frost obtained. The dog did not know anything about thermometers. Possibly in its brain there was no sharp consciousness of a condition of very cold such as was in the man's brain. But the brute had its instinct. It experienced a vague but menacing apprehension that subdued it and made it slink along at the man's heels, and that made it question eagerly every unwonted movement of the man as if expecting him to go into camp or to seek shelter somewhere and build a fire. The dog had learned fire, and it wanted fire, or else to burrow under the snow and cuddle its warmth away from the air.

The frozen moisture of its breathing had settled on its fur in a fine powder of frost, and especially were its jowls, muzzle, and eyelashes whitened by its crystalled breath. The man's red beard and moustache were likewise frosted, but more solidly, the deposit taking the form of ice and increasing with every warm, moist breath he exhaled. Also, the man was chewing tobacco, and the muzzle of ice held his lips so rigidly that he was unable to clear his chin when he expelled the juice. The result was that a crystal beard of the colour and solidity of amber was increasing its length on his chin. If he fell down it would shatter itself, like glass, into brittle fragments. But he did not mind the appendage. It was the penalty all tobacco-chewers paid in that country, and he had been out before in two cold snaps. They had not been so cold as this, he knew, but by the spirit thermometer at Sixty Mile he knew they had been registered at fifty below and at fifty-five.

He held on through the level stretch of woods for several miles, crossed a wide flat of nigger-heads, and dropped down a bank to the frozen bed of a small stream. This was Henderson Creek, and he knew he was ten miles from the forks. He looked at his watch. It was ten o'clock. He was making four miles an hour, and he calculated that he would arrive at the forks at half-past twelve. He decided to celebrate that event by eating his lunch there.

The dog dropped in again at his heels, with a tail drooping discouragement, as the man swung along the creek-bed. The furrow of the old sled-trail was plainly visible, but a dozen inches of snow covered the marks of the last runners. In a month no man had come up or down that silent creek. The man held steadily on. He was not much given to thinking, and just then particularly he had nothing to think about save that he would eat lunch at the forks and that at six o'clock he would be in camp with the boys. There was nobody to talk to and, had there been, speech would have been impossible because of the ice-muzzle on his mouth. So he continued monotonously to chew tobacco and to increase the length of his amber beard.

Once in a while the thought reiterated itself that it was very cold and that he had never experienced such cold. As he walked along he rubbed his cheek-bones and nose with the back of his mittened hand. He did this automatically, now and again changing hands. But rub as he would, the instant he stopped his cheek-bones went numb, and the following instant the end of his nose went numb. He was sure to frost his cheeks; he knew that, and experienced a pang of regret that he had not devised a nose-strap of the sort Bud wore in cold snaps. Such a strap passed across the cheeks, as well, and saved them. But it didn't matter much, after all. What were frosted cheeks? A bit painful, that was all; they were never serious.

Empty as the man's mind was of thoughts, he was keenly observant, and he noticed the changes in the creek, the curves and bends and timber-jams, and always he sharply noted where he placed his feet. Once, coming around a bend, he shied abruptly, like a startled horse, curved away from the place where he had been walking, and retreated several paces back along the trail. The creek he knew was frozen clear to the bottom—no creek could contain water in that arctic winter—but he knew also that there were springs that bubbled out from the hillsides and ran along under the snow and on top the ice of the creek. He knew that the coldest snaps never froze these springs, and he knew likewise their danger. They were traps. They hid pools of water under the snow that might be three inches deep, or three feet. Sometimes a skin of ice half an inch thick covered them, and in turn was covered by the snow. Sometimes there were alternate layers of water and ice-skin, so that when one broke through he kept on breaking through for a while, sometimes wetting himself to the waist.

That was why he had shied in such panic. He had felt the give under his feet and heard the crackle of a snow-hidden ice-skin. And to get his feet wet in such a temperature meant trouble and danger. At the very least it meant delay, for he would be forced to stop and build a fire, and under its protection to bare his feet while he dried his socks and moccasins. He stood and studied the creek-bed and its banks, and decided that the flow of water came from the right. He reflected awhile, rubbing his nose and cheeks, then skirted to the left, stepping gingerly and testing the footing for each step. Once clear of the danger, he took a fresh chew of tobacco and swung along at his four-mile gait.

In the course of the next two hours he came upon several similar traps. Usually the snow above the hidden pools had a sunken, candied appearance that advertised the danger. Once again, however, he had a close call; and once, suspecting danger, he compelled the dog to go on in front. The dog did not want to go. It hung back until the man shoved it forward, and then it went quickly across the white, unbroken surface. Suddenly it broke through, floundered to one side, and got away to firmer footing. It had wet its forefeet and legs, and almost immediately the water that clung to it turned to ice. It made quick efforts to lick the ice off its legs, then dropped down in the snow and began to bite out the ice that had formed between the toes. This was a matter of instinct. To permit the ice to remain would mean sore feet. It did not know this. It merely obeyed the mysterious prompting that arose from the deep crypts of its being. But the man knew, having achieved a judgment on the subject, and he removed the mitten from his right hand and helped tear out the ice-particles. He did not expose his fingers more than a minute, and was astonished at the swift numbness that smote them. It certainly was cold. He pulled on the mitten hastily, and beat the hand savagely across his chest.

At twelve o'clock the day was at its brightest. Yet the sun was too far south on its winter journey to clear the horizon. The bulge of the earth intervened between it and Henderson Creek, where the man walked under a clear sky at noon and cast no shadow. At half-past twelve, to the minute, he arrived at the forks of the creek. He was pleased at the speed he had made. If he kept it up, he would certainly be with the boys by six. He unbuttoned his jacket and shirt and drew forth his lunch. The action consumed no more than a quarter of a minute, yet in that brief moment the numbness laid hold of the exposed fingers. He did not put the mitten on, but, instead, struck the fingers a dozen sharp smashes against his leg. Then he sat down on a snow-covered log to eat. The sting that followed upon the striking of his fingers against his leg ceased so quickly that he was startled, he had had no chance to take a bite of biscuit. He struck the fingers repeatedly and returned them to the mitten, baring the other hand for the purpose of eating. He tried to take a mouthful, but the ice-muzzle prevented. He had forgotten to build a fire and thaw out. He chuckled at his foolishness, and as he chuckled he noted the numbness creeping into the exposed fingers. Also, he noted that the stinging which had first come to his toes when he sat down was already passing away. He wondered whether the toes were warm or numbed. He moved them inside the moccasins and decided that they were numbed.

He pulled the mitten on hurriedly and stood up. He was a bit frightened. He stamped up and down until the stinging returned into the feet. It certainly was cold, was his thought. That man from Sulphur Creek had spoken the truth when telling how cold it sometimes got in the country. And he had laughed at him at the time! That showed one must not be too sure of things. There was no mistake about it, it was cold. He strode up and down, stamping his feet and threshing his arms, until reassured by the returning warmth. Then he got out matches and proceeded to make a fire. From the undergrowth, where high water of the previous spring had lodged a supply of seasoned twigs, he got his firewood. Working carefully from a small beginning, he soon had a roaring fire, over which he thawed the ice from his face and in the protection of which he ate his biscuits. For the moment the cold of space was outwitted. The dog took satisfaction in the fire, stretching out close enough for warmth and far enough away to escape being singed.

When the man had finished, he filled his pipe and took his comfortable time over a smoke. Then he pulled on his mittens, settled the ear-flaps of his cap firmly about his ears, and took the creek trail up the left fork. The dog was disappointed and yearned back toward the fire. This man did not know cold. Possibly all the generations of his ancestry had been ignorant of cold, of real cold, of cold one hundred and seven degrees below freezing-point. But the dog knew; all its ancestry knew, and it had inherited the knowledge. And it knew that it was not good to walk abroad in such fearful cold. It was the time to lie snug in a hole in the snow and wait for a curtain of cloud to be drawn across the face of outer space whence this cold came. On the other hand, there was keen intimacy between the dog and the man. The one was the toil-slave of the other, and the only caresses it had ever received were the caresses of the whip-lash and of harsh and menacing throat-sounds that threatened the whip-lash. So the dog made no effort to communicate its apprehension to the man. It was not concerned in the welfare of the man; it was for its own sake that it yearned back toward the fire. But the man whistled, and spoke to it with the sound of whip-lashes, and the dog swung in at the man's heels and followed after.

The man took a chew of tobacco and proceeded to start a new amber beard. Also, his moist breath quickly powdered with white his moustache, eyebrows, and lashes. There did not seem to be so many springs on the left fork of the Henderson, and for half an hour the man saw no signs of any. And then it happened. At a place where there were no signs, where the soft, unbroken snow seemed to advertise solidity beneath, the man broke through. It was not deep. He wetted himself half-way to the knees before he floundered out to the firm crust.

He was angry, and cursed his luck aloud. He had hoped to get into camp with the boys at six o'clock, and this would delay him an hour, for he would have to build a fire and dry out his foot-gear. This was imperative at that low temperature—he knew that much; and he turned aside to the bank, which he climbed. On top, tangled in the underbrush about the trunks of several small spruce trees, was a high-water deposit of dry firewood—sticks and twigs principally, but also larger portions of seasoned branches and fine, dry, last-year's grasses. He threw down several large pieces on top of the snow. This served for a foundation and prevented the young flame from drowning itself in the snow it otherwise would melt. The flame he got by touching a match to a small shred of birch-bark that he took from his pocket. This burned even more readily than paper. Placing it on the foundation, he fed the young flame with wisps of dry grass and with the tiniest dry twigs.

He worked slowly and carefully, keenly aware of his danger. Gradually, as the flame grew stronger, he increased the size of the twigs with which he fed it. He squatted in the snow, pulling the twigs out from their entanglement in the brush and feeding directly to the flame. He knew there must be no failure. When it is seventy-five below zero, a man must not fail in his first attempt to build a fire—that is, if his feet are wet. If his feet are dry, and he fails, he can run along the trail for half a mile and restore his circulation. But the circulation of wet and freezing feet cannot be restored by running when it is seventy-five below. No matter how fast he runs, the wet feet will freeze the harder.

All this the man knew. The old-timer on Sulphur Creek had told him about it the previous fall, and now he was appreciating the advice. Already all sensation had gone out of his feet. To build the fire he had been forced to remove his mittens, and the fingers had quickly gone numb. His pace of four miles an hour had kept his heart pumping blood to the surface of his body and to all the extremities. But the instant he stopped, the action of the pump eased down. The cold of space smote the unprotected tip of the planet, and he, being on that unprotected tip, received the full force of the blow. The blood of his body recoiled before it. The blood was alive, like the dog, and like the dog it wanted to hide away and cover itself up from the fearful cold. So long as he walked four miles an hour, he pumped that blood, willy-nilly, to the surface; but now it ebbed away and sank down into the recesses of his body. The extremities were the first to feel its absence. His wet feet froze the faster, and his exposed fingers numbed the faster, though they had not yet begun to freeze. Nose and cheeks were already freezing, while the skin of all his body chilled as it lost its blood.

But he was safe. Toes and nose and cheeks would be only touched by the frost, for the fire was beginning to burn with strength. He was feeding it with twigs the size of his finger. In another minute he would be able to feed it with branches the size of his wrist, and then he could remove his wet foot-gear, and, while it dried, he could keep his naked feet warm by the fire, rubbing them at first, of course, with snow. The fire was a success. He was safe. He remembered the advice of the old-timer on Sulphur Creek, and smiled. The old-timer had been very serious in laying down the law that no man must travel alone in the Klondike after fifty below. Well, here he was; he had had the accident; he was alone; and he had saved himself. Those old-timers were rather womanish, some of them, he thought. All a man had to do was to keep his head, and he was all right. Any man who was a man could travel alone. But it was surprising, the rapidity with which his cheeks and nose were freezing. And he had not thought his fingers could go lifeless in so short a time. Lifeless they were, for he could scarcely make them move together to grip a twig, and they seemed remote from his body and from him. When he touched a twig, he had to look and see whether or not he had hold of it. The wires were pretty well down between him and his finger-ends.

All of which counted for little. There was the fire, snapping and crackling and promising life with every dancing flame. He started to untie his moccasins. They were coated with ice; the thick German socks were like sheaths of iron half-way to the knees; and the mocassin strings were like rods of steel all twisted and knotted as by some conflagration. For a moment he tugged with his numbed fingers, then, realizing the folly of it, he drew his sheath-knife.

But before he could cut the strings, it happened. It was his own fault or, rather, his mistake. He should not have built the fire under the spruce tree. He should have built it in the open. But it had been easier to pull the twigs from the brush and drop them directly on the fire. Now the tree under which he had done this carried a weight of snow on its boughs. No wind had blown for weeks, and each bough was fully freighted. Each time he had pulled a twig he had communicated a slight agitation to the tree—an imperceptible agitation, so far as he was concerned, but an agitation sufficient to bring about the disaster. High up in the tree one bough capsized its load of snow. This fell on the boughs beneath, capsizing them. This process continued, spreading out and involving the whole tree. It grew like an avalanche, and it descended without warning upon the man and the fire, and the fire was blotted out! Where it had burned was a mantle of fresh and disordered snow.

The man was shocked. It was as though he had just heard his own sentence of death. For a moment he sat and stared at the spot where the fire had been. Then he grew very calm. Perhaps the old-timer on Sulphur Creek was right. If he had only had a trail-mate he would have been in no danger now. The trail-mate could have built the fire. Well, it was up to him to build the fire over again, and this second time there must be no failure. Even if he succeeded, he would most likely lose some toes. His feet must be badly frozen by now, and there would be some time before the second fire was ready.

Such were his thoughts, but he did not sit and think them. He was busy all the time they were passing through his mind, he made a new foundation for a fire, this time in the open; where no treacherous tree could blot it out. Next, he gathered dry grasses and tiny twigs from the high-water flotsam. He could not bring his fingers together to pull them out, but he was able to gather them by the handful. In this way he got many rotten twigs and bits of green moss that were undesirable, but it was the best he could do. He worked methodically, even collecting an armful of the larger branches to be used later when the fire gathered strength. And all the while the dog sat and watched him, a certain yearning wistfulness in its eyes, for it looked upon him as the fire-provider, and the fire was slow in coming.

When all was ready, the man reached in his pocket for a second piece of birch-bark. He knew the bark was there, and, though he could not feel it with his fingers, he could hear its crisp rustling as he fumbled for it. Try as he would, he could not clutch hold of it. And all the time, in his consciousness, was the knowledge that each instant his feet were freezing. This thought tended to put him in a panic, but he fought against it and kept calm. He pulled on his mittens with his teeth, and threshed his arms back and forth, beating his hands with all his might against his sides. He did this sitting down, and he stood up to do it; and all the while the dog sat in the snow, its wolf-brush of a tail curled around warmly over its forefeet, its sharp wolf-ears pricked forward intently as it watched the man. And the man as he beat and threshed with his arms and hands, felt a great surge of envy as he regarded the creature that was warm and secure in its natural covering.

After a time he was aware of the first far-away signals of sensation in his beaten fingers. The faint tingling grew stronger till it evolved into a stinging ache that was excruciating, but which the man hailed with satisfaction. He stripped the mitten from his right hand and fetched forth the birch-bark. The exposed fingers were quickly going numb again. Next he brought out his bunch of sulphur matches. But the tremendous cold had already driven the life out of his fingers. In his effort to separate one match from the others, the whole bunch fell in the snow. He tried to pick it out of the snow, but failed. The dead fingers could neither touch nor clutch. He was very careful. He drove the thought of his freezing feet; and nose, and cheeks, out of his mind, devoting his whole soul to the matches. He watched, using the sense of vision in place of that of touch, and when he saw his fingers on each side the bunch, he closed them—that is, he willed to close them, for the wires were drawn, and the fingers did not obey. He pulled the mitten on the right hand, and beat it fiercely against his knee. Then, with both mittened hands, he scooped the bunch of matches, along with much snow, into his lap. Yet he was no better off.

After some manipulation he managed to get the bunch between the heels of his mittened hands. In this fashion he carried it to his mouth. The ice crackled and snapped when by a violent effort he opened his mouth. He drew the lower jaw in, curled the upper lip out of the way, and scraped the bunch with his upper teeth in order to separate a match. He succeeded in getting one, which he dropped on his lap. He was no better off. He could not pick it up. Then he devised a way. He picked it up in his teeth and scratched it on his leg. Twenty times he scratched before he succeeded in lighting it. As it flamed he held it with his teeth to the birch-bark. But the burning brimstone went up his nostrils and into his lungs, causing him to cough spasmodically. The match fell into the snow and went out.

The old-timer on Sulphur Creek was right, he thought in the moment of controlled despair that ensued: after fifty below, a man should travel with a partner. He beat his hands, but failed in exciting any sensation. Suddenly he bared both hands, removing the mittens with his teeth. He caught the whole bunch between the heels of his hands. His arm-muscles not being frozen enabled him to press the hand-heels tightly against the matches. Then he scratched the bunch along his leg. It flared into flame, seventy sulphur matches at once! There was no wind to blow them out. He kept his head to one side to escape the strangling fumes, and held the blazing bunch to the birch-bark. As he so held it, he became aware of sensation in his hand. His flesh was burning. He could smell it. Deep down below the surface he could feel it. The sensation developed into pain that grew acute. And still he endured it, holding the flame of the matches clumsily to the bark that would not light readily because his own burning hands were in the way, absorbing most of the flame.

At last, when he could endure no more, he jerked his hands apart. The blazing matches fell sizzling into the snow, but the birch-bark was alight. He began laying dry grasses and the tiniest twigs on the flame. He could not pick and choose, for he had to lift the fuel between the heels of his hands. Small pieces of rotten wood and green moss clung to the twigs, and he bit them off as well as he could with his teeth. He cherished the flame carefully and awkwardly. It meant life, and it must not perish. The withdrawal of blood from the surface of his body now made him begin to shiver, and he grew more awkward. A large piece of green moss fell squarely on the little fire. He tried to poke it out with his fingers, but his shivering frame made him poke too far, and he disrupted the nucleus of the little fire, the burning grasses and tiny twigs separating and scattering. He tried to poke them together again, but in spite of the tenseness of the effort, his shivering got away with him, and the twigs were hopelessly scattered. Each twig gushed a puff of smoke and went out. The fire-provider had failed. As he looked apathetically about him, his eyes chanced on the dog, sitting across the ruins of the fire from him, in the snow, making restless, hunching movements, slightly lifting one forefoot and then the other, shifting its weight back and forth on them with wistful eagerness.

The sight of the dog put a wild idea into his head. He remembered the tale of the man, caught in a blizzard, who killed a steer and crawled inside the carcass, and so was saved. He would kill the dog and bury his hands in the warm body until the numbness went out of them. Then he could build another fire. He spoke to the dog, calling it to him; but in his voice was a strange note of fear that frightened the animal, who had never known the man to speak in such way before. Something was the matter, and its suspicious nature sensed danger—it knew not what danger but somewhere, somehow, in its brain arose an apprehension of the man. It flattened its ears down at the sound of the man's voice, and its restless, hunching movements and the liftings and shiftings of its forefeet became more pronounced but it would not come to the man. He got on his hands and knees and crawled toward the dog. This unusual posture again excited suspicion, and the animal sidled mincingly away.

The man sat up in the snow for a moment and struggled for calmness. Then he pulled on his mittens, by means of his teeth, and got upon his feet. He glanced down at first in order to assure himself that he was really standing up, for the absence of sensation in his feet left him unrelated to the earth. His erect position in itself started to drive the webs of suspicion from the dog's mind; and when he spoke peremptorily, with the sound of whip-lashes in his voice, the dog rendered its customary allegiance and came to him. As it came within reaching distance, the man lost his control. His arms flashed out to the dog, and he experienced genuine surprise when he discovered that his hands could not clutch, that there was neither bend nor feeling in the fingers. He had forgotten for the moment that they were frozen and that they were freezing more and more. All this happened quickly, and before the animal could get away, he encircled its body with his arms. He sat down in the snow, and in this fashion held the dog, while it snarled and whined and struggled.

But it was all he could do, hold its body encircled in his arms and sit there. He realized that he could not kill the dog. There was no way to do it. With his helpless hands he could neither draw nor hold his sheath-knife nor throttle the animal. He released it, and it plunged wildly away, with tail between its legs, and still snarling. It halted forty feet away and surveyed him curiously, with ears sharply pricked forward. The man looked down at his hands in order to locate them, and found them hanging on the ends of his arms. It struck him as curious that one should have to use his eyes in order to find out where his hands were. He began threshing his arms back and forth, beating the mittened hands against his sides. He did this for five minutes, violently, and his heart pumped enough blood up to the surface to put a stop to his shivering. But no sensation was aroused in the hands. He had an impression that they hung like weights on the ends of his arms, but when he tried to run the impression down, he could not find it.

A certain fear of death, dull and oppressive, came to him. This fear quickly became poignant as he realized that it was no longer a mere matter of freezing his fingers and toes, or of losing his hands and feet, but that it was a matter of life and death with the chances against him. This threw him into a panic, and he turned and ran up the creek-bed along the old, dim trail. The dog joined in behind and kept up with him. He ran blindly, without intention, in fear such as he had never known in his life. Slowly, as he ploughed and floundered through the snow, he began to see things again—the banks of the creek, the old timber-jams, the leafless aspens, and the sky. The running made him feel better. He did not shiver. Maybe, if he ran on, his feet would thaw out; and, anyway, if he ran far enough, he would reach camp and the boys. Without doubt he would lose some fingers and toes and some of his face; but the boys would take care of him, and save the rest of him when he got there. And at the same time there was another thought in his mind that said he would never get to the camp and the boys; that it was too many miles away, that the freezing had too great a start on him, and that he would soon be stiff and dead. This thought he kept in the background and refused to consider. Sometimes it pushed itself forward and demanded to be heard, but he thrust it back and strove to think of other things.

It struck him as curious that he could run at all on feet so frozen that he could not feel them when they struck the earth and took the weight of his body. He seemed to himself to skim along above the surface and to have no connection with the earth. Somewhere he had once seen a winged Mercury, and he wondered if Mercury felt as he felt when skimming over the earth.

His theory of running until he reached camp and the boys had one flaw in it: he lacked the endurance. Several times he stumbled, and finally he tottered, crumpled up, and fell. When he tried to rise, he failed. He must sit and rest, he decided, and next time he would merely walk and keep on going. As he sat and regained his breath, he noted that he was feeling quite warm and comfortable. He was not shivering, and it even seemed that a warm glow had come to his chest and trunk. And yet, when he touched his nose or cheeks, there was no sensation. Running would not thaw them out. Nor would it thaw out his hands and feet. Then the thought came to him that the frozen portions of his body must be extending. He tried to keep this thought down, to forget it, to think of something else; he was aware of the panicky feeling that it caused, and he was afraid of the panic. But the thought asserted itself, and persisted, until it produced a vision of his body totally frozen. This was too much, and he made another wild run along the trail. Once he slowed down to a walk, but the thought of the freezing extending itself made him run again.

And all the time the dog ran with him, at his heels. When he fell down a second time, it curled its tail over its forefeet and sat in front of him facing him curiously eager and intent. The warmth and security of the animal angered him, and he cursed it till it flattened down its ears appeasingly. This time the shivering came more quickly upon the man. He was losing in his battle with the frost. It was creeping into his body from all sides. The thought of it drove him on, but he ran no more than a hundred feet, when he staggered and pitched headlong. It was his last panic. When he had recovered his breath and control, he sat up and entertained in his mind the conception of meeting death with dignity. However, the conception did not come to him in such terms. His idea of it was that he had been making a fool of himself, running around like a chicken with its head cut off—such was the simile that occurred to him. Well, he was bound to freeze anyway, and he might as well take it decently. With this new-found peace of mind came the first glimmerings of drowsiness. A good idea, he thought, to sleep off to death. It was like taking an anaesthetic. Freezing was not so bad as people thought. There were lots worse ways to die.

He pictured the boys finding his body next day. Suddenly he found himself with them, coming along the trail and looking for himself. And, still with them, he came around a turn in the trail and found himself lying in the snow. He did not belong with himself any more, for even then he was out of himself, standing with the boys and looking at himself in the snow. It certainly was cold, was his thought. When he got back to the States he could tell the folks what real cold was. He drifted on from this to a vision of the old-timer on Sulphur Creek. He could see him quite clearly, warm and comfortable, and smoking a pipe.

"You were right, old hoss; you were right," the man mumbled to the old-timer of Sulphur Creek.

Then the man drowsed off into what seemed to him the most comfortable and satisfying sleep he had ever known. The dog sat facing him and waiting. The brief day drew to a close in a long, slow twilight. There were no signs of a fire to be made, and, besides, never in the dog's experience had it known a man to sit like that in the snow and make no fire. As the twilight drew on, its eager yearning for the fire mastered it, and with a great lifting and shifting of forefeet, it whined softly, then flattened its ears down in anticipation of being chidden by the man. But the man remained silent. Later, the dog whined loudly. And still later it crept close to the man and caught the scent of death. This made the animal bristle and back away. A little longer it delayed, howling under the stars that leaped and danced and shone brightly in the cold sky. Then it turned and trotted up the trail in the direction of the camp it knew, where were the other food-providers and fire-providers.

TIPS FOR THE TRAIL

First Aid - Snake Bite

Wear high leather boots and long pants in snake country. Most snakes are not poisonous but unless you know for sure, treat the bite as dangerous. Ideally, the victim should get to medical help for anti-venom, but you need to administer first aid in the field.

1. Remove rings and jewelry around the bitten area.
2. Stay calm and ensure that the victim remains calm.
3. The victim should lie down with the bitten area lower than the rest of his body.
4. If you have a venom extractor, you can apply it within the first 3 minutes of the bite. Do not use your mouth to suck out the venom. DO NOT CUT THE SKIN! This is not recommended anymore due to danger of infection.
5. Treat for shock. Don't apply ice nor use a tourniquet.
6. Get the victim to medical help as soon as possible.

TIPS FOR THE TRAIL

What to Do...Around Bears

There are some general guidelines about what to do if a bear approaches. None of these are foolproof or guaranteed, but they might help. Every situation is going to be different.

Avoid the problem

- Avoid problems in the first place by not leaving food around your camp and safely storing it at night in bear-safe storage away from camp. This involves either using a special bear cannister, or hanging the food from a tree. This also keeps the food away from smaller animals, like raccoons and skunks. Cannisters are really the only effective method since bears can climb trees and chew through lines holding food bags (Trust me on this--it has happened to me.) and they may be required.
- Don't keep food of any kind, including food wrappers or toothpaste, in your tent. Don't cook in your tent.
- Burn food scraps and containers in your fire. Pack out what's left.
- If hiking, make noise as you walk to avoid coming upon a bear and startling it. Try talking or singing, or carry jangling bells.

If a bear approaches

- Don't run or try to climb a tree. Stay calm and in place and face the bear. If with others, stay as a group.
- Don't block the bear's escape route or come between a mother bear and her cubs. Give the bear some space.
- Shouting or making noise may cause the bear to depart.
- Keep facing the bear but don't fall down or play dead yet.
- If a grizzly(brown) bear attacks, do not fight back but play dead and use your hands to protect your neck.
- If a black bear attacks, you should normally fight back by kicking, hitting with a stick, etc.
- If the bear comes close, use pepper spray if you have it.

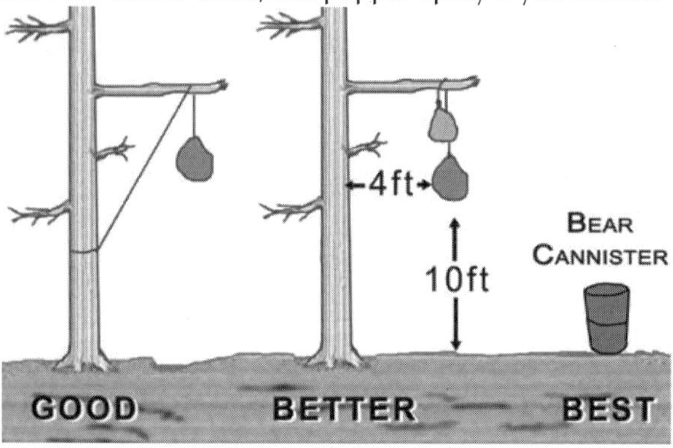

Buck Pulls A Thousand Pounds

From *The Call of the Wild*
by Jack London

That winter, at Dawson, Buck performed another exploit, not so heroic, perhaps, but one that put his name many notches higher on the totem-pole of Alaskan fame. This exploit was particularly gratifying to the three men; for they stood in need of the outfit which it furnished, and were enabled to make a long-desired trip into the virgin East, where miners had not yet appeared. It was brought about by a conversation in the Eldorado Saloon, in which men waxed boastful of their favorite dogs. Buck, because of his record, was the target for these men, and Thornton was driven stoutly to defend him. At the end of half an hour one man stated that his dog could start a sled with five hundred pounds and walk off with it; a second bragged six hundred for his dog; and a third, seven hundred.

"Pooh! pooh!" said John Thornton; "Buck can start a thousand pounds."

"And break it out? and walk off with it for a hundred yards?" demanded Matthewson, a Bonanza King, he of the seven hundred vaunt.

"And break it out, and walk off with it for a hundred yards," John Thornton said coolly.

"Well," Matthewson said, slowly and deliberately, so that all could hear, "I've got a thousand dollars that says he can't. And there it is." So saying, he slammed a sack of gold dust of the size of a bologna sausage down upon the bar.

Nobody spoke. Thornton's bluff, if bluff it was, had been called. He could feel a flush of warm blood creeping up his face. His tongue had tricked him. He did not know whether Buck could start a thousand pounds. Half a ton! The enormousness of it appalled him. He had great faith in Buck's strength and had often thought him capable of starting such a load; but never, as now, had he faced the possibility of it, the eyes of a dozen men fixed upon him, silent and waiting. Further, he had no thousand dollars; nor had Hans or Pete.

"I've got a sled standing outside now, with twenty fifty-pound sacks of flour on it," Matthewson went on with brutal directness; "so don't let that hinder you."

Thornton did not reply. He did not know what to say. He glanced from face to face in the absent way of a man who has lost the power of thought and is seeking somewhere to find the thing that will start it going again. The face of Jim O'Brien, a Mastodon King and old-time comrade, caught his eyes. It was as a cue to him, seeming to rouse him to do what he would never have dreamed of doing.

"Can you lend me a thousand?" he asked, almost in a whisper.

"Sure," answered O'Brien, thumping down a plethoric sack by the side of Matthewson's. "Though it's little faith I'm having, John, that the beast can do the trick."

The Eldorado emptied its occupants into the street to see the test. The tables were deserted, and the dealers and gamekeepers came forth to see the outcome of the wager and to lay odds. Several hundred men, furred and mittened, banked around the sled within easy distance. Matthewson's sled, loaded with a thousand pounds of flour, had been standing for a couple of hours, and in the intense cold (it was sixty below zero) the runners had frozen fast to the hard-packed snow. Men offered odds of two to one that Buck could not budge the sled. A quibble arose concerning the phrase "break out." O'Brien contended it was Thornton's privilege to knock the runners loose, leaving Buck to "break it out" from a dead standstill. Matthewson insisted that the phrase included breaking the runners from the frozen grip of the snow. A majority of the men who had witnessed the making of the bet decided in his favor, whereat the odds went up to three to one against Buck.

There were no takers. Not a man believed him capable of the feat. Thornton had been hurried into the wager, heavy with doubt; and now that he looked at the sled itself, the concrete fact, with the regular team of ten dogs curled up in the snow before it, the more impossible the task appeared. Matthewson waxed jubilant.

"Three to one!" he proclaimed. "I'll lay you another thousand at that figure, Thornton. What d'ye say?"

Thornton's doubt was strong in his face, but his fighting spirit was aroused—the fighting spirit that soars above odds, fails to recognize the impossible, and is deaf to all save the clamor for battle. He called Hans and Pete to him. Their sacks were slim, and with his own the three partners could rake together only two hundred dollars. In the ebb of their fortunes, this sum was their total capital; yet they laid it unhesitatingly against Matthewson's six hundred.

The team of ten dogs was unhitched, and Buck, with his own harness, was put into the sled. He had caught the contagion of the excitement, and he felt that in some way he must do a great thing for John Thornton. Murmurs of admiration at his splendid appearance went up. He was in perfect condition, without an ounce of superfluous flesh, and the one hundred and fifty pounds that he weighed were so many pounds of grit and virility. His furry coat shone with the sheen of silk. Down the neck and across the shoulders, his mane, in repose as it was, half bristled and seemed to lift with every movement, as though excess of vigor made each particular hair alive and active. The great breast and heavy fore legs were no more than in proportion with the rest of the body, where the muscles showed in tight rolls underneath the skin. Men felt these muscles and proclaimed them hard as iron, and the odds went down to two to one.

"Gad, sir! Gad, sir!" stuttered a member of the latest dynasty, a king of the Skookum Benches. "I offer you eight hundred for him, sir, before the test, sir; eight hundred just as he stands." Thornton shook his head and stepped to Buck's side. "You must stand off from him," Matthewson protested. "Free play and plenty of room."

The crowd fell silent; only could be heard the voices of the gamblers vainly offering two to one. Everybody acknowledged Buck a magnificent animal, but twenty fifty-pound sacks of flour bulked too large in their eyes for them to loosen their pouch-strings.

Thornton knelt down by Buck's side. He took his head in his two hands and rested cheek on cheek. He did not playfully shake him, as was his wont, or murmur soft love curses; but he whispered in his ear. "As you love me, Buck. As you love me," was what he whispered. Buck whined with suppressed eagerness.

The crowd was watching curiously. The affair was growing mysterious. It seemed like a conjuration. As Thornton got to his feet, Buck seized his mittened hand between his jaws, pressing in with his teeth and releasing slowly, half-reluctantly. It was the answer, in terms, not of speech, but of love. Thornton stepped well back.

"Now, Buck," he said. Buck tightened the traces, then slacked them for a matter of several inches. It was the way he had learned. "Gee!" Thornton's voice rang out, sharp in the tense silence. Buck swung to the right, ending the movement in a plunge that took up the slack and with a sudden jerk arrested his one hundred and fifty pounds. The load quivered, and from under the runners arose a crisp crackling.

"Haw!" Thornton commanded.

Buck duplicated the manoeuvre, this time to the left. The crackling turned into a snapping, the sled pivoting and the runners slipping and grating several inches to the side. The sled was broken out. Men were holding their breaths, intensely unconscious of the fact.

"Now, MUSH!"

Thornton's command cracked out like a pistol-shot. Buck threw himself forward, tightening the traces with a jarring lunge. His whole body was gathered compactly together in the tremendous effort, the muscles writhing and knotting like live things under the silky fur. His great chest was low to the ground, his head forward and down, while his feet were flying like mad, the claws scarring the hard-packed snow in parallel grooves. The sled swayed and trembled, half-started forward. One of his feet slipped, and one man groaned aloud. Then the sled lurched ahead in what appeared a rapid succession of jerks, though it never really came to a dead stop again ...half an inch... an inch . . . two inches. . . The jerks perceptibly diminished; as the sled gained momentum, he caught them up, till it was moving steadily along.

Men gasped and began to breathe again, unaware that for a moment they had ceased to breathe. Thornton was running behind, encouraging Buck with short, cheery words. The distance had been measured off, and as he neared the pile of firewood which marked the end of the hundred yards, a cheer began to grow and grow, which burst into a roar as he passed the firewood and halted at command. Every man was tearing himself loose, even Matthewson.

Hats and mittens were flying in the air. Men were shaking hands, it did not matter with whom, and bubbling over in a general incoherent babel.

But Thornton fell on his knees beside Buck. Head was against head, and he was shaking him back and forth. Those who hurried up heard him cursing Buck, and he cursed him long and fervently, and softly and lovingly.

"Gad, sir! Gad, sir!" spluttered the Skookum Bench king. "I'll give you a thousand for him, sir, a thousand, sir—twelve hundred, sir."

Thornton rose to his feet. His eyes were wet. The tears were streaming frankly down his cheeks. "Sir," he said to the Skookum Bench king, "no, sir. You can go to hell, sir. It's the best I can do for you, sir."

Buck seized Thornton's hand in his teeth. Thornton shook him back and forth. As though animated by a common impulse, the onlookers drew back to a respectful distance; nor were they again indiscreet enough to interrupt.

TIPS FOR THE TRAIL

Navigation - Telling Time at Night

Impress your friends by having 3 ways to tell the time at night using only your brain and things found in your tent.

First, you can use the position of the Big Dipper, knowing the day of the year.

1. On January 8 at 5:00am, the Big Dipper two pointer stars form a vertical line above the North Star. Take today's date and subtract 2 hours of time from 5:00am for every month after January 8. That will be the time that the two pointer stars are vertical for today - it may be in the middle of the day.

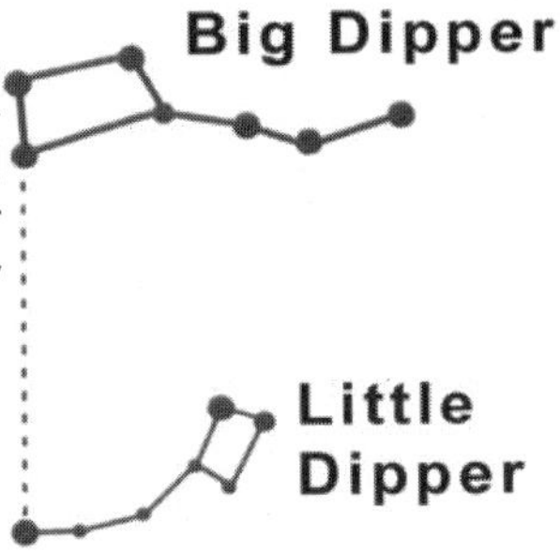

Jan 8	5am	Jul 8	5pm
Feb 8	3am	Aug 8	3pm
Mar 8	1am	Sep 8	1pm
Apr 8	11pm	Oct 8	11am
May 8	9pm	Nov 8	9am
Jun 8	7pm	Dec 8	7am

2. Now, observe the location of the pointer stars right now and calculate the difference between their location and straight up, using the chart at the right. You will notice that every hour of angle is equal to 2 hours of time.

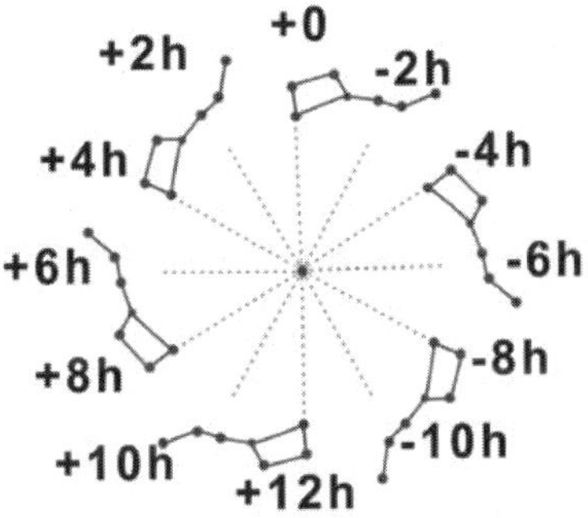

3. Take the difference you calculated in the last step and add or subtract that from the time you calculated in step 1. This is local time, which would then have to be adjusted for your longitude and daylight savings to get a more exact time.

The second way works better later in the night. Take a metal object like a pot or cup and align it vertically. Then, start banging it on the tent pole. Assuming you are not camping alone, fairly soon someone else will supply the time by yelling something like, "Hey, shut up! Don't you know it is 2:30 in the morning?" No corrections to this time are required.

The third way...turn on your flashlight and look at your watch.

South

Excerpts from *The Story of Shackleton's Last Expedition 1914-1917* by Sir Ernest Shackleton

Sir Ernest Shackleton set out in 1914 on an expedition to reach the South Pole. Almost abandoned with the onset of World War I, the expedition was permitted to continue by the British government. His ship, *Endurance*, became stuck in the ice before reaching her destination and finally sank 10 months later. The men lived on the ship until she sank, then lived on ice floes for five months before setting out in their lifeboats to Elephant Island. Shackleton and a small party then set out in a boat to find help which they eventually secured. In one of the most hostile environments on earth, Shackleton was able to keep his party together and bring them all to safety—a most amazing accomplishment. The following is a synopsis of that trip up to the point where the rescue party reaches South Georgia Island. The remainder of the crew at Elephant Island were rescued shortly thereafter.

STUCK IN THE ICE

On February 24 we ceased to observe ship routine, and the *Endurance* became a winter station. All hands were on duty during the day and slept at night, except a watchman who looked after the dogs and watched for any sign of movement in the ice. We cleared a space of 10 ft. by 20 ft. round the rudder and propeller, sawing through ice 2 ft. thick, and lifting the blocks with a pair of tongs made by the carpenter.

The drift of the *Endurance* in the grip of the pack continued without incident of importance through June. A faint twilight round about noon of each day reminded us of the sun, and assisted us in the important work of exercising the dogs.

The most severe blizzard we had experienced in the Weddell Sea swept down upon the *Endurance* on the evening of the 13th, and by breakfast-time on the following morning the kennels to the windward, or southern side of the ship, were buried under 5 ft. of drift. The ship was invisible at a distance of fifty yards, and it was impossible to preserve one's sense of direction in the raging wind and suffocating drift. To walk against the gale was out of the question. Face and eyes became snowed up within two minutes, and serious frost-bites would have been the penalty of perseverance. The dogs stayed in their kennels for the most part, the "old stagers" putting out a paw occasionally in order to keep open a breathing-hole. By evening the gale had attained a force of 60 or 70 miles an hour, and the ship was trembling under the attack. At least 100 tons of snow were piled against the bows and port side, where the weight of the drift had forced the floe downward. The temperature during the blizzard had ranged from -21° to -33.5° F.

The break-up of our floe came suddenly on Sunday, August 1, just one year after the *Endurance* left the South-West India Docks on the voyage to the Far South. I had the dogs and sledges brought aboard at once and the gangway hoisted. The pressure was cracking the floe rapidly, rafting it close to the ship and forcing masses of ice beneath the keel. I had the boats cleared away ready for lowering, got up some additional stores, and set a double watch. All hands were warned to stand by, get what sleep they could, and have their warmest clothing at hand. The *Endurance* had been built to withstand the attacks of the ice, and she lifted bravely as the floes drove beneath her. The effects of the pressure around us were awe-inspiring. Mighty blocks of ice, gripped between meeting floes, rose slowly till they jumped like cherry-stones squeezed between thumb and finger. The pressure of millions of tons of moving ice was crushing and smashing inexorably. If the ship was once gripped firmly her fate would be sealed.

The gale from the south-west blew all night and moderated during the afternoon of the 2nd to a stiff breeze. The rudder had been driven hard over to starboard and the blade partially torn away from the rudder-head. Heavy masses of ice were still jammed against the stern, and it was impossible to ascertain the extent of the damage at that time.

LOSS OF THE *ENDURANCE*

The next attack of the ice came on the afternoon of October 18th. The two floes began to move laterally, exerting great pressure on the ship. Suddenly the floe on the port side cracked and huge pieces of ice shot up from under the port bilge. Within a few seconds the ship heeled over until she had a list of thirty degrees to port, being held under the starboard bilge by the opposing floe. The lee boats were now almost resting on the floe. The midship dog-kennels broke away and crashed down on to the lee kennels, and the howls and barks of the frightened dogs assisted to create a perfect pandemonium. Everything movable on deck and below fell to the lee side, and for a few minutes it looked as if the *Endurance* would be thrown upon her beam ends. Order was soon restored. I had all fires put out and battens nailed on the deck to give the dogs a foothold and enable people to get about. Then the crew lashed all the movable gear. If the ship had heeled any farther it would have been necessary to release the lee boats and pull them clear, and Worsley was watching to give the alarm. At 8 p.m. the floes opened, and within a few minutes the *Endurance* was nearly upright again. Orders were given for the ice to be chipped clear of the rudder. The men poled the blocks out of the way when they had been detached from the floe with the long ice-chisels, and we were able to haul the ship's stern into a clear berth. An uproar among the dogs attracted attention late in the afternoon, and we found a 25-ft. whale cruising up and down in our pool. It pushed its head up once in characteristic killer fashion, but we judged from its small curved dorsal fin that it was a specimen of Balaenoptera acutorostrata, not Orca gladiator.

I had the pumps rigged, got up steam, and started the bilge-pumps at 8 p.m. The pressure by that time had relaxed. The ship was making water rapidly aft, and the carpenter set to work to make a coffer-dam astern of the engines. All hands worked, watch and watch, throughout the night, pumping ship and helping the carpenter. By morning the leak was being kept in check. The carpenter and his assistants caulked the coffer-dam with strips of blankets and nailed strips over the seams wherever possible. The main or hand pump was frozen up and could not be used at once.

The following day brought bright clear weather, with a blue sky. The sunshine was inspiriting. The roar of pressure could be heard all around us. New ridges were rising, and I could see as the day wore on that the lines of major disturbance were drawing nearer to the ship. The *Endurance* suffered some strains at intervals. Listening below, I could hear the creaking and groaning of her timbers, the pistol-like cracks that told of the starting of a trenail or plank, and the faint, indefinable whispers of our ship's distress. The butts of planking were opened four and five inches on the starboard side, and at the same time we could see from the bridge that the ship was bending like a bow under titanic pressure. Almost like a living creature, she resisted the forces that would crush her; but it was a one-sided battle. Millions of tons of ice pressed inexorably upon the little ship that had dared the challenge of the Antarctic. The *Endurance* was now leaking badly, and at 9 p.m. I gave the order to lower boats, gear, provisions, and sledges to the floe, and move them to the flat ice a little way from the ship. The working of the ice closed the leaks slightly at midnight, but all hands were pumping all night. A strange occurrence was the sudden appearance of eight emperor penguins from a crack 100 yds. away at the moment when the pressure upon the ship was at its climax. They walked a little way towards us, halted, and after a few ordinary calls proceeded to utter weird cries that sounded like a dirge for the ship.

The attack of the ice reached its climax at 4 p.m. The ship was hove stern up by the pressure, and the driving floe, moving laterally across the stern, split the rudder and tore out the rudder- post and stern-post. Then, while we watched, the ice loosened and the *Endurance* sank a little. The decks were breaking upwards and the water was puring in below. Again the pressure began, and at 5 p.m. I ordered all hands on to the ice. It was a sickening sensation to feel the decks breaking up under one's feet, the great beams bending and then snapping with a noise like heavy gunfire. The water was overmastering the pumps, and to avoid an explosion when it reached the boilers I had to give orders for the fires to be drawn and the steam let down. The plans for abandoning the ship in case of emergency had been made well in advance, and men and dogs descended to the floe and made their way to the comparative safety of an unbroken portion of the floe without a hitch.

Essential supplies had been placed on the floe about 100 yds. from the ship, and there we set about making a camp for the night. But about 7 p.m., after the tents were up, the ice we were occupying became involved in the pressure and started to split and smash beneath our feet. I had the camp moved to a bigger floe about 200 yds. away, just beyond the bow of the ship. Boats, stores, and camp equipment had to be conveyed across a working pressure-ridge.

After the tents had been pitched I mustered all hands and explained the position to them briefly and, I hope, clearly. I have told them the distance to the Barrier and the distance to Paulet Island, and have stated that I propose to try to march with equipment across the ice in the direction of Paulet Island. I thanked the men for the steadiness and good morale they have shown in these trying circumstances, and told them I had no doubt that, provided they continued to work their utmost and to trust me, we will all reach safety in the end.

At midnight I was pacing the ice, listening to the grinding floe and to the groans and crashes that told of the death-agony of the *Endurance*, when I noticed suddenly a crack running across our floe right through the camp. The alarm-whistle brought all hands tumbling out, and we moved the tents and stores lying on what was now the smaller portion of the floe to the larger portion. Nothing more could be done at that moment, and the men turned in again; but there was little sleep. Each time I came to the end of my beat on the floe I could just see in the darkness the uprearing piles of pressure-ice, which toppled over and narrowed still further the little floating island we occupied. All night long the electric light gleamed from the stern of the dying *Endurance*. Hussey had left this light switched on when he took a last observation, and, like a lamp in a cottage window, it braved the night until in the early morning the *Endurance* received a particularly violent squeeze. There was a sound of rending beams and the light disappeared. The connexion had been cut.

The cook prepared breakfast, which consisted of biscuit and hoosh, at 8 a.m., and I then went over to the *Endurance* again and made a fuller examination of the wreck. Only six of the cabins had not been pierced by floes and blocks of ice. Every one of the starboard cabins had been crushed. The whole of the after part of the ship had been crushed concertina fashion. The forecastle and the Ritz were submerged, and the wardroom was three-quarters full of ice. The starboard side of the wardroom had come away. The motor-engine forward had been driven through the galley. Petrol-cases that had been stacked on the fore-deck had been driven by the floe through the wall into the wardroom and had carried before them a large picture. Curiously enough, the glass of this picture had not been cracked, whereas in the immediate neighbourhood I saw heavy iron davits that had been twisted and bent like the ironwork of a wrecked train. The ship was being crushed remorselessly.

AT OCEAN CAMP

Next day broke cold and still with the same wet snow. Taking into account also the possibility of leads opening close to us, and so of our being able to row north-west to where we might find land, I decided to find a more solid floe and there camp until conditions were more favourable for us to make an attempt to escape from our icy prison. To this end we moved our tents and all our gear to a thick, heavy old floe about one and a half miles from the wreck and there made our camp. We called this "Ocean Camp." It was with the utmost difficulty that we shifted our two boats. The surface was terrible--like nothing that any of us had ever seen around us before. We were sinking at times up to our hips, and everywhere the snow was two feet deep.

A party was sent back to Dump Camp, near the ship, to collect as much clothing, tobacco, etc., as they could find. The remainder of the men made themselves as comfortable as possible under the circumstances at Ocean Camp. This floating lump of ice, about a mile square at first but later splitting into smaller and smaller fragments, was to be our home for nearly two months.

The two subjects of most interest to us were our rate of drift and the weather. Our hope, of course, was to drift northwards to the edge of the pack and then, when the ice was loose enough, to take to the boats and row to the nearest land. We started off in fine style, drifting north about twenty miles in two or three days in a howling south-westerly blizzard. Gradually, however, we slowed up, as successive observations showed, until we began to drift back to the south. An increasing north-easterly wind, which commenced on November 7 and lasted for twelve days, damped our spirits for a time, until we found that we had only drifted back to the south three miles, so that we were now seventeen miles to the good.

The temperature still continued to rise, reaching 33°F. on November 14. The thaw consequent upon these high temperatures was having a disastrous effect upon the surface of our camp. "The surface is awful!--not slushy, but elusive. You step out gingerly. All is well for a few paces, then your foot suddenly sinks a couple of feet until it comes to a hard layer. You wade along in this way step by step, like a mudlark at Portsmouth Hard, hoping gradually to regain the surface. Soon you do, only to repeat the exasperating performance ad lib., to the accompaniment of all the expletives that you can bring to bear on the subject. What actually happens is that the warm air melts the surface sufficiently to cause drops of water to trickle down slightly, where, on meeting colder layers of snow, they freeze again, forming a honeycomb of icy nodules instead of the soft, powdery, granular snow that we are accustomed to.

I had already made arrangements for a quick move in case of a sudden break-up of the ice. Emergency orders were issued; each man had his post allotted and his duty detailed; and the whole was so organized that in less than five minutes from the sounding of the alarm on my whistle, tents were struck, gear and provisions packed, and the whole party was ready to move off. It was with a feeling almost of relief that the end came.

November 21, 1915—This evening, as we were lying in our tents we heard the Boss call out, 'She's going, boys!' We were out in a second and up on the look-out station and other points of vantage, and, sure enough, there was our poor ship a mile and a half away struggling in her death-agony. She went down bows first, her stern raised in the air. She then gave one quick dive and the ice closed over her for ever. It gave one a sickening sensation to see it, for, mastless and useless as she was, she seemed to be a link with the outer world. Without her our destitution seems more emphasized, our desolation more complete. The loss of the ship sent a slight wave of depression over the camp. No one said much, but we cannot be blamed for feeling it in a sentimental way. I doubt if there was one amongst us who did not feel some personal emotion when Sir Ernest, standing on the top of the look-out, said somewhat sadly and quietly, 'She's gone, boys.'

On December 20, after discussing the question with Wild, I informed all hands that I intended to try and make a march to the west to reduce the distance between us and Paulet Island. A buzz of pleasurable anticipation went round the camp, and every one was anxious to get on the move. So the next day I set off with Wild, Crean, and Hurley, with dog teams, to the westward to survey the route. After travelling about seven miles we mounted a small berg, and there as far as we could see stretched a series of immense flat floes from half a mile to a mile across, separated from each other by pressure-ridges which seemed easily negotiable with pick and shovel. The only place that appeared likely to be formidable was a very much cracked-up area between the old floe that we were on and the first of the series of young flat floes about half a mile away.

By this time blubber was a regular article of our diet—either raw, boiled, or fried. "It is remarkable how our appetites have changed in this respect. Until quite recently almost the thought of it was nauseating. Now, however, we positively demand it. The thick black oil which is rendered down from it, rather like train-oil in appearance and cod-liver oil in taste, we drink with avidity."

Our meals were now practically all seal meat, with one biscuit at midday; and I calculated that at this rate, allowing for a certain number of seals and penguins being caught, we could last for nearly six months. We were all very weak though, and as soon as it appeared likely that we should leave our floe and take to the boats, I should have to considerably increase the ration. One day a huge sea-leopard climbed on to the floe and attacked one of the men. Wild, hearing the shouting, ran out and shot it. When it was cut up, we found in its stomach several undigested fish. These we fried in some of its blubber, and so had our only "fresh" fish meal during the whole of our drift on the ice.

"As fuel is so scarce we have had to resort to melting ice for drinking-water in tins against our bodies, and we treat the tins of dog-pemmican for breakfast similarly by keeping them in our sleeping-bags all night."

"The temperature was not strikingly low as temperatures go down here, but the terrific winds penetrate the flimsy fabric of our fragile tents and create so much draught that it is impossible to keep warm within. At supper last night our drinking-water froze over in the tin in the tent before we could drink it. It is curious how thirsty we all are."

Our hopes were now centred on Elephant Island or Clarence Island, which lay 100 miles almost due north of us.

ESCAPE FROM THE ICE

"We still have the dark water-sky of the last week with us to the south-west and west, round to the north-east. We are leaving all the bergs to the west and there are few within our range of vision now. The swell is more marked to-day, and I feel sure we are at the verge of the floe-ice. One strong gale, followed by a calm would scatter the pack, I think, and then we could push through. I have been thinking much of our prospects. The appearance of Clarence Island after our long drift seems, somehow, to convey an ultimatum. The island is the last outpost of the south and our final chance of a landing-place. Beyond it lies the broad Atlantic. Our little boats may be compelled any day now to sail unsheltered over the open sea with a thousand leagues of ocean separating them from the land to the north and east. It seems vital that we shall land on Clarence Island or its neighbour, Elephant Island. The latter island has attraction for us, although as far as I know nobody has ever landed there. Its name suggests the presence of the plump and succulent sea-elephant. We have an increasing desire in any case to get firm ground under our feet. The floe has been a good friend to us, but it is reaching the end of its journey, and it is liable at any time now to break up and fling us into the unplumbed sea."

At 6.30 p.m. a particularly heavy shock went through our floe. The watchman and other members of the party made an immediate inspection and found a crack right under the *James Caird* and between the other two boats and the main camp. Within five minutes the boats were over the crack and close to the tents. The trouble was not caused by a blow from another floe. We could see that the piece of ice we occupied had slewed and now presented its long axis towards the oncoming swell. The floe, therefore, was pitching in the manner of a ship, and it had cracked across when the swell lifted the centre, leaving the two ends comparatively unsupported. We were now on a triangular raft of ice, the three sides measuring, roughly, 90, 100, and 120 yds. Night came down dull and overcast, and before midnight the wind had freshened from the west. We could see that the pack was opening under the influence of wind, wave, and current, and I felt that the time for launching the boats was near at hand. Indeed, it was obvious that even if the conditions were unfavourable for a start during the coming day, we could not safely stay on the floe many hours longer. The movement of the ice in the swell was increasing, and the floe might split right under our camp. We had made preparations for quick action if anything of the kind occurred. Our case would be desperate if the ice broke into small pieces not large enough to support our party and not loose enough to permit the use of the boats.

Soon after breakfast the ice closed again. We were standing by, with our preparations as complete as they could be made, when at 11 a.m. our floe suddenly split right across under the boats. We rushed our gear on to the larger of the two pieces and watched with strained attention for the next development. The crack had cut through the site of my tent. I stood on the edge of the new fracture, and, looking across the widening channel of water, could see the spot where for many months my head and shoulders had rested when I was in my sleeping-bag. The depression formed by my body and legs was on our side of the crack. The ice had sunk under my weight during the months of waiting in the tent, and I had many times put snow under the bag to fill the hollow. The lines of stratification showed clearly the different layers of snow. How fragile and precarious had been our resting-place! Yet usage had dulled our sense of danger. The floe had become our home, and during the early months of the drift we had almost ceased to realize that it was but a sheet of ice floating on unfathomed seas. Now our home was being shattered under our feet, and we had a sense of loss and incompleteness hard to describe.

The call to action came at 1 p.m. The pack opened well and the channels became navigable. The conditions were not all one could have desired, but it was best not to wait any longer. The *Dudley Docker* and the *Stancomb Wills* were launched quickly. Stores were thrown in, and the two boats were pulled clear of the immediate floes towards a pool of open water three miles broad, in which floated a lone and mighty berg. The *James Caird* was the last boat to leave, heavily loaded with stores and odds and ends of camp equipment. Many things regarded by us as essentials at that time were to be discarded a little later as the pressure of the primitive became more severe. Man can sustain life with very scanty means.

The three boats were a mile away from our floe home at 2 p.m. We had made our way through the channels and had entered the big pool when we saw a rush of foam-clad water and tossing ice approaching us, like the tidal bore of a river. The pack was being impelled to the east by a tide-rip, and two huge masses of ice were driving down upon us on converging courses. The *James Caird* was leading. Starboarding the helm and bending strongly to the oars, we managed to get clear. The two other boats followed us, though from their position astern at first they had not realized the immediate danger. The *Stancomb Wills* was the last boat and she was very nearly caught, but by great exertion she was kept just ahead of the driving ice. It was an unusual and startling experience. The effect of tidal action on ice is not often as marked as it was that day. The advancing ice, accompanied by a large wave, appeared to be travelling at about three knots; and if we had not succeeded in pulling clear we would certainly have been swamped.

We pulled hard for an hour to windward of the berg that lay in the open water. The swell was crashing on its perpendicular sides and throwing spray to a height of sixty feet. Evidently there was an ice-foot at the east end, for the swell broke before it reached the berg-face and flung its white spray on to the blue ice-wall. We might have paused to have admired the spectacle under other conditions; but night was coming on apace, and we needed a camping-place. As we steered north-west, still amid the ice-floes, the *Dudley Docker* got jammed between two masses while attempting to make a short cut. The old adage about a short cut being the longest way round is often as true in the

Antarctic as it is in the peaceful countryside. The *James Caird* got a line aboard the *Dudley Docker*, and after some hauling the boat was brought clear of the ice again. We hastened forward in the twilight in search of a flat, old floe, and presently found a fairly large piece rocking in the swell. It was not an ideal camping-place by any means, but darkness had overtaken us. We hauled the boats up, and by 8 p.m. had the tents pitched and the blubber-stove burning cheerily. Soon all hands were well fed and happy in their tents, and snatches of song came to me as I wrote up my log.

Some intangible feeling of uneasiness made me leave my tent about 11 p.m. that night and glance around the quiet camp. The stars between the snow-flurries showed that the floe had swung round and was end on to the swell, a position exposing it to sudden strains. I started to walk across the floe in order to warn the watchman to look carefully for cracks, and as I was passing the men's tent the floe lifted on the crest of a swell and cracked right under my feet. The men were in one of the dome-shaped tents, and it began to stretch apart as the ice opened. A muffled sound, suggestive of suffocation, came from beneath the stretching tent. I rushed forward, helped some emerging men from under the canvas, and called out, "Are you all right?"

"There are two in the water," somebody answered. The crack had widened to about four feet, and as I threw myself down at the edge, I saw a whitish object floating in the water. It was a sleeping-bag with a man inside. I was able to grasp it, and with a heave lifted man and bag on to the floe. A few seconds later the ice-edges came together again with tremendous force. Fortunately, there had been but one man in the water, or the incident might have been a tragedy. The rescued bag contained Holness, who was wet down to the waist but otherwise unscathed. The crack was now opening again. The *James Caird* and my tent were on one side of the opening and the remaining two boats and the rest of the camp on the other side. With two or three men to help me I struck my tent; then all hands manned the painter and rushed the *James Caird* across the opening crack. We held to the rope while, one by one, the men left on our side of the floe jumped the channel or scrambled over by means of the boat. Finally I was left alone. The night had swallowed all the others and the rapid movement of the ice forced me to let go the painter. For a moment I felt that my piece of rocking floe was the loneliest place in the world. Peering into the darkness; I could just see the dark figures on the other floe. I hailed Wild, ordering him to launch the *Stancomb Wills*, but I need not have troubled. His quick brain had anticipated the order and already the boat was being manned and hauled to the ice-edge. Two or three minutes later she reached me, and I was ferried across to the Camp.

We were now on a piece of flat ice about 200 ft. long and 100 ft. wide. There was no more sleep for any of us that night. The killer whales were blowing in the lanes around, and we waited for daylight and watched for signs of another crack in the ice. The hours passed with laggard feet as we stood huddled together or walked to and fro in the effort to keep some warmth in our bodies. We lit the blubber-stove at 3 a.m., and with pipes going and a cup of hot milk for each man, we were able to discover some bright spots in our outlook. At any rate, we were on the move at last, and if dangers and difficulties lay ahead we could meet and overcome them. No longer were we drifting helplessly at the mercy of wind and current.

Our chance came at 8, when we launched the boats, loaded them, and started to make our way through the lanes in a northerly direction. The *James Caird* was in the lead, with the *Stancomb Wills* next and the *Dudley Docker* bringing up the rear. In order to make the boats more seaworthy we had left some of our shovels, picks, and dried vegetables on the floe, and for a long time we could see the abandoned stores forming a dark spot on the ice. The boats were still heavily loaded. We got out of the lanes, and entered a stretch of open water at 11 a.m. A strong easterly breeze was blowing, but the fringe of pack lying outside protected us from the full force of the swell, just as the coral-reef of a tropical island checks the rollers of the Pacific. Our way was across the open sea, and soon after noon we swung round the north end of the pack and laid a course to the westward, the *James Caird* still in the lead. Immediately our deeply laden boats began to make heavy weather. They shipped sprays, which, freezing as they fell, covered men and gear with ice, and soon it was clear that we could not safely proceed. I put the *James Caird* round and ran for the shelter of the pack again, the other boats following. Back inside the outer line of ice the sea was not breaking. This was at 3 p.m., and all hands were tired and cold. A big floeberg resting peacefully ahead caught my eye, and half an hour later we had hauled up the boats and pitched camp for the night. It was a fine, big, blue berg with an attractively solid appearance, and from our camp we could get a good view of the surrounding sea and ice. The highest point was about 15 ft. above sea- level. After a hot meal all hands, except the watchman, turned in. Every one was in need of rest after the troubles of the previous night and the unaccustomed strain of the last thirty-six hours at the oars. The berg appeared well able to withstand the battering of the sea, and too deep and massive to be seriously affected by the swell; but it was not as safe as it looked. About midnight the watchman called me and showed me that the heavy north-westerly swell was undermining the ice. A great piece had broken off within eight feet of my tent. We made what inspection was possible in the darkness, and found that on the westward side of the berg the thick snow covering was yielding rapidly to the attacks of the sea. An ice-foot had formed just under the surface of the water.

Other articles of our scanty equipment had to go the next night. We were carrying only the things that had seemed essential, but we stripped now to the barest limit of safety. Constant rain and snow squalls blotted out the stars and soaked us through, and at times it was only by shouting to each other that we managed to keep the boats together. There was no sleep for anybody owing to the severe cold, and we dare not pull fast enough to keep ourselves warm since we were unable to see more than a few yards ahead. Occasionally the ghostly shadows of silver, snow, and fulmar petrels flashed close to us, and all around we could hear the killers blowing, their short, sharp hisses sounding like sudden escapes of steam. The killers were a source of anxiety, for a boat could easily have been capsized by one of them coming up to blow. They would throw aside in a nonchalant fashion pieces of ice much bigger than our boats when they rose to the surface, and we had an uneasy feeling that the white bottoms of the boats would look like ice from below.

We made our way through the lanes till at noon we were suddenly spewed out of the pack into the open ocean. Dark blue and sapphire green ran the seas. Our sails were soon up, and with a fair wind we moved over the waves like three Viking ships on the quest of a lost Atlantis. With the sheet well out and the sun shining bright above, we enjoyed for a few hours a sense of the freedom and magic of the sea, compensating us for pain and trouble in the days that had passed. At last we were free from the ice, in water that our boats could navigate.

During the afternoon we had to take a second reef in the sails, for the wind freshened and the deeply laden boats were shipping much water and steering badly in the rising sea. I had laid the course for Elephant Island and we were making good progress. The *Dudley Docker* ran down to me at dusk and Worsley suggested that we should stand on all night; but already the *Stancomb Wills* was barely discernible among the rollers in the gathering dusk, and I decided that it would be safer to heave to and wait for the daylight. It would never have done for the boats to have become separated from one another during the night. The party must be kept together, and, moreover, I thought it possible that we might overrun our goal in the darkness and not be able to return. So we made a sea-anchor of oars and hove to, the *Dudley Docker* in the lead, since she had the longest painter. The *James Caird* swung astern of the *Dudley Docker* and the *Stancomb Wills* again had the third place. We ate a cold meal and did what little we could to make things comfortable for the hours of darkness. Rest was not for us. During the greater part of the night the sprays broke over the boats and froze in masses of ice, especially at the stern and bows. This ice had to be broken away in order to prevent the boats growing too heavy. The temperature was below zero and the wind penetrated our clothes and chilled us almost unbearably. I doubted if all the men would survive that night. One of our troubles was lack of water. We had emerged so suddenly from the pack into the open sea that we had not had time to take aboard ice for melting in the cookers, and without ice we could not have hot food. The *Dudley Docker* had one lump of ice weighing about ten pounds, and this was shared out among all hands. We sucked small pieces and got a little relief from thirst engendered by the salt spray, but at the same time we reduced our bodily heat. The condition of most of the men was pitiable. All of us had swollen mouths and we could hardly touch the food. One of the people on the *Stancomb Wills* shouted, "We are doing all right, but I would like some dry mitts." The jest brought a smile to cracked lips. He might as well have asked for the moon. The only dry things aboard the boats were swollen mouths and burning tongues. Thirst is one of the troubles that confront the traveller in polar regions. Ice may be plentiful on every hand, but it does not become drinkable until it is melted, and the amount that may be dissolved in the mouth is limited. We had been thirsty during the days of heavy pulling in the pack, and our condition was aggravated quickly by the salt spray. Our sleeping-bags would have given us some warmth, but they were not within our reach. They were packed under the tents in the bows, where a mail-like coating of ice enclosed them, and we were so cramped that we could not pull them out.

At last daylight came, and with the dawn the weather cleared and the wind fell to a gentle south-westerly breeze. A magnificent sunrise heralded in what we hoped would be our last day in the boats. Rose-pink in the growing light, the lofty peak of Clarence Island told of the coming glory of the sun. The sky grew blue above us and the crests of the waves sparkled cheerfully. As soon as it was light enough we chipped and scraped the ice off the bows and sterns. The rudders had been unshipped during the night in order to avoid the painters catching them. We cast off our ice-anchor and pulled the oars aboard. They had grown during the night to the thickness of telegraph-poles while rising and falling in the freezing seas, and had to be chipped clear before they could be brought inboard.

We were dreadfully thirsty now. We found that we could get momentary relief by chewing pieces of raw seal meat and swallowing the blood, but thirst came back with redoubled force owing to the saltness of the flesh. I gave orders, therefore, that meat was to be served out only at stated intervals during the day or when thirst seemed to threaten the reason of any particular individual. In the full daylight Elephant Island showed cold and severe to the north-north-west. The island was on the bearings that Worsley had laid down, and I congratulated him on the accuracy of his navigation under difficult circumstances, with two days dead reckoning while following a devious course through the pack- ice and after drifting during two nights at the mercy of wind and waves.

ELEPHANT ISLAND

Progress was slow, but gradually Elephant Island came nearer and soon we were next to the island. All this time we were coasting along beneath towering rocky cliffs and sheer glacier-faces, which offered not the slightest possibility of landing anywhere. At 9.30 a.m. we spied a narrow, rocky beach at the base of some very high crags and cliff, and made for it. To our joy, we sighted the *James Caird* and the *Stancomb Wills* sailing into the same haven just ahead of us. We were so delighted that we gave three cheers, which were not heard aboard the other boats owing to the roar of the surf. However, we soon joined them and were able to exchange experiences on the beach.

Rowing carefully and avoiding the blind rollers which showed where sunken rocks lay, we brought the *Stancomb Wills* towards the opening in the reef. Then, with a few strong strokes we shot through on the top of a swell and ran the boat on to a stony beach. The next swell lifted her a little farther. This was the first landing ever made on Elephant Island, and a thought came to me that the honour should belong to the youngest member of the Expedition, so I told Blackborrow to jump over. He seemed to be in a state almost of coma, and in order to avoid delay I helped him, perhaps a little roughly, over the side of the boat. He promptly sat down in the surf and did not move. Then I suddenly realized what I had forgotten, that both his feet were frost-bitten badly. Some of us jumped over and pulled him into a dry place. It was a rather rough experience for Blackborrow, but, anyhow, he is now able to say that he was the first man to sit on Elephant Island. Possibly at the time he would have been willing to forgo any distinction of the kind.

A curious spectacle met my eyes when I landed the second time. Some of the men were reeling about the beach as if they had found an unlimited supply of alcoholic liquor on the desolate shore. They were laughing uproariously, picking up stones and letting handfuls of pebbles trickle between their fingers like misers gloating over hoarded gold. The smiles and laughter, which caused cracked lips to bleed afresh, and the gleeful exclamations at the sight of two live seals on the beach made me think for a moment of that glittering hour of childhood when the door is open at last and the Christmas-tree in all its wonder bursts upon the vision.

Soon half a dozen of us had the stores ashore. Our strength was nearly exhausted and it was heavy work carrying our goods over the rough pebbles and rocks to the foot of the cliff, but we dare not leave anything within reach of the tide. We had to wade knee-deep in the icy water in order to lift the gear from the boats. When the work was done we pulled the three boats a little higher on the beach and turned gratefully to enjoy the hot drink the cook had prepared. Those of us who were comparatively fit had to wait until the weaker members of the party had been supplied; but every man had his pannikin of hot milk in the end, and never did anything taste better. Seal steak and blubber followed, for the seals that had been careless enough to await our arrival on the beach had already given up their lives.

The snow had made it impossible for us to find the tide-line and we were uncertain how far the sea was going to encroach upon our beach. I pitched my tent on the seaward side of the camp so that I might have early warning of danger, and, sure enough, about 2 a.m. a little wave forced its way under the tent- cloth. This was a practical demonstration that we had not gone far enough back from the sea, but in the semi-darkness it was difficult to see where we could find safety. Perhaps it was fortunate that experience had inured us to the unpleasantness of sudden forced changes of camp. We took down the tents and re-pitched them close against the high rocks at the seaward end of the spit, where large boulders made an uncomfortable resting-place. Snow was falling heavily. Then all hands had to assist in pulling the boats farther up the beach, and at this task we suffered a serious misfortune. Two of our four bags of clothing had been placed under the bilge of the *James Caird*, and before we realized the danger a wave had lifted the boat and carried the two bags back into the surf. We had no chance of recovering them. This accident did not complete the tale of the night's misfortunes. The big eight-man tent was blown to pieces in the early morning. Some of the men who had occupied it took refuge in other tents, but several remained in their sleeping-bags under the fragments of cloth until it was time to turn out.

The weather was still bad on the morning of April 19. Some of the men were showing signs of demoralization. They were disinclined to leave the tents when the hour came for turning out, and it was apparent they were thinking more of the discomforts of the moment than of the good fortune that had brought us to sound ground and comparative safety. The condition of the gloves and headgear shown me by some discouraged men illustrated the proverbial carelessness of the sailor. The articles had frozen stiff during the night, and the owners considered, it appeared, that this state of affairs provided them with a grievance, or at any rate gave them the right to grumble. They said they wanted dry clothes and that their health would not admit of their doing any work. Only by rather drastic methods were they induced to turn to. Frozen gloves and helmets undoubtedly are very uncomfortable, and the proper thing is to keep these articles thawed by placing them inside one's shirt during the night.

THE BOAT JOURNEY

A boat journey in search of relief was necessary and must not be delayed. That conclusion was forced upon me. The nearest port where assistance could certainly be secured was Port Stanley, in the Falkland Islands, 540 miles away, but we could scarcely hope to beat up against the prevailing north-westerly wind in a frail and weakened boat with a small sail area. South Georgia was over 800 miles away, but lay in the area of the west winds, and I could count upon finding whalers at any of the whaling-stations on the east coast. A boat party might make the voyage and be back with relief within a month, provided that the sea was clear of ice and the boat survive the great seas. It was not difficult to decide that South Georgia must be the objective, and I proceeded to plan ways and means. The hazards of a boat journey across 800 miles of stormy sub-Antarctic ocean were obvious, but I calculated that at worst the venture would add nothing to the risks of the men left on the island. There would be fewer mouths to feed during the winter and the boat would not require to take more than one month's provisions for six men, for if we did not make South Georgia in that time we were sure to go under. A consideration that had weight with me was that there was no chance at all of any search being made for us on Elephant Island.

There was a lull in the bad weather on April 21, and the carpenter started to collect material for the decking of the *James Caird*. He fitted the mast of the *Stancomb Wills* fore and aft inside the *James Caird* as a hog-back and thus strengthened the keel with the object of preventing our boat "hogging"--that is, buckling in heavy seas. He had not sufficient wood to provide a deck, but by using the sledge- runners and box-lids he made a framework extending from the forecastle aft to a well. It was a patched-up affair, but it provided a base for a canvas covering. We had a bolt of canvas frozen stiff, and this material had to be cut and then thawed out over the blubber-stove, foot by foot, in order that it might be sewn into the form of a cover. When it had been nailed and screwed into position it certainly gave an appearance of safety to the boat, though I had an uneasy feeling that it bore a strong likeness to stage scenery, which may look like a granite wall and is in fact nothing better than canvas and lath. As events proved, the covering served its purpose well. We certainly could not have lived through the voyage without it.

Our last night on the solid ground of Elephant Island was cold and uncomfortable. We turned out at dawn and had breakfast. Then we launched the *Stancomb Wills* and loaded her with stores, gear, and ballast, which would be transferred to the *James Caird* when the heavier boat had been launched. The ballast consisted of bags made from blankets and filled with sand, making a total weight of about 1000 lbs. In addition we had gathered a number of round boulders and about 250 lbs. of ice, which would supplement our two casks of water.

By midday the *James Caird* was ready for the voyage. Vincent and the carpenter had secured some dry clothes by exchange with members of the shore party (I heard afterwards that it was a full fortnight before the soaked garments were finally dried), and the boat's crew was standing by waiting for the order to cast off. Then we pushed off for the last time, and within a few minutes I was aboard the *James Caird*. The crew of the *Stancomb Wills* shook hands with us as the boats bumped together and offered us the last good wishes. Then, setting our jib, we cut the painter and moved away to the north-east. The men who were staying behind made a pathetic little group on the beach, with the grim heights of the island behind them and the sea seething at their feet, but they waved to us and gave three hearty cheers. There was hope in their hearts and they trusted us to bring the help that they needed.

I had all sails set, and the *James Caird* quickly dipped the beach and its line of dark figures. The westerly wind took us rapidly to the line of pack, and as we entered it I stood up with my arm around the mast, directing the steering, so as to avoid the great lumps of ice that were flung about in the heave of the sea. The pack thickened and we were forced to turn almost due east, running before the wind towards a gap I had seen in the morning from the high ground. I could not see the gap now, but we had come out on its bearing and I was prepared to find that it had been influenced by the easterly drift. At four o'clock in the afternoon we found the channel, much narrower than it had seemed in the morning but still navigable. Dropping sail, we rowed through without touching the ice anywhere, and by 5.30 p.m. we were clear of the pack with open water before us. We passed one more piece of ice in the darkness an hour later, but the pack lay behind, and with a fair wind swelling the sails we steered our little craft through the night, our hopes centred on our distant goal. The swell was very heavy now, and when the time came for our first evening meal we found great difficulty in keeping the Primus lamp alight and preventing the hoosh splashing out of the pot. Three men were needed to attend to the cooking, one man holding the lamp and two men guarding the aluminium cooking-pot, which had to be lifted clear of the Primus whenever the movement of the boat threatened to cause a disaster. Then the lamp had to be protected from water, for sprays were coming over the bows and our flimsy decking was by no means water-tight. All these operations were conducted in the confined space under the decking, where the men lay or knelt and adjusted themselves as best they could to the angles of our cases and ballast. It was uncomfortable, but we found consolation in the reflection that without the decking we could not have used the cooker at all.

The tale of the next sixteen days is one of supreme strife amid heaving waters. The sub-Antarctic Ocean lived up to its evil winter reputation. I decided to run north for at least two days while the wind held and so get into warmer weather before turning to the east and laying a course for South Georgia. We took two-hourly spells at the tiller. The men who were not on watch crawled into the sodden sleeping-bags and tried to forget their troubles for a period; but there was no comfort in the boat. The bags and cases seemed to be alive in the unfailing knack of presenting their most uncomfortable angles to our rest-seeking bodies. A man might imagine for a moment that he had found a position of ease, but always discovered quickly that some unyielding point was impinging on muscle or bone. The first night aboard the boat was one of acute discomfort for us all, and we were heartily glad when the dawn came and we could set about the preparation of a hot breakfast.

There were no dry places in the boat, and at last we simply covered our heads with our Burberrys and endured the all-pervading water. The baling was work for the watch. Real rest we had none. The perpetual motion of the boat made repose impossible; we were cold, sore, and anxious. We moved on hands and knees in the semi-darkness of the day under the decking. The darkness was complete by 6 p.m., and not until 7 a.m. of the following day could we see one another under the thwarts. We had a few scraps of candle, and they were preserved carefully in order that we might have light at meal-times. There was one fairly dry spot in the boat, under the solid original decking at the bows, and we managed to protect some of our biscuit from the salt water; but I do not think any of us got the taste of salt out of our mouths during the voyage.

While a new watch was shivering in the wind and spray, the men who had been relieved groped hurriedly among the soaked sleeping-bags and tried to steal a little of the warmth created by the last occupants; but it was not always possible for us to find even this comfort when we went off watch. The boulders that we had taken aboard for ballast had to be shifted continually in order to trim the boat and give access to the pump, which became choked with hairs from the moulting sleeping-bags and finneskoe. The four reindeer-skin sleeping-bags shed their hair freely owing to the continuous wetting, and soon became quite bald in appearance.

On the tenth night Worsley could not straighten his body after his spell at the tiller. He was thoroughly cramped, and we had to drag him beneath the decking and massage him before he could unbend himself and get into a sleeping-bag. At midnight I was at the tiller and suddenly noticed a line of clear sky between the south and south-west. I called to the other men that the sky was clearing, and then a moment later I realized that what I had seen was not a rift in the clouds but the white crest of an enormous wave. During twenty-six years' experience of the ocean in all its moods I had not encountered a wave so gigantic. It was a mighty upheaval of the ocean, a thing quite apart from the big white-capped seas that had been our tireless enemies for many days. I shouted, "For God's sake, hold on! It's got us!" Then came a moment of suspense that seemed drawn out into hours. White surged the foam of the breaking sea around us. We felt our boat lifted and flung forward like a cork in breaking surf. We were in a seething chaos of tortured water; but somehow the boat lived through it, half-full of water, sagging to the dead weight and shuddering under the blow. We baled with the energy of men fighting for life, flinging the water over the sides with every receptacle that came to our hands, and after ten minutes of uncertainty we felt the boat renew her life beneath us. She floated again and ceased to lurch drunkenly as though dazed by the attack of the sea. Earnestly we hoped that never again would we encounter such a wave.

The conditions in the boat, uncomfortable before, had been made worse by the deluge of water. All our gear was thoroughly wet again. Our cooking-stove had been floating about in the bottom of the boat, and portions of our last hoosh seemed to have permeated everything. Not until 3 a.m., when we were all chilled almost to the limit of endurance, did we manage to get the stove alight and make ourselves hot drinks.

Several days later, at 12.30 p.m., through a rift in the clouds, McCarthy caught a glimpse of the black cliffs of South Georgia, just fourteen days after our departure from Elephant Island. It was a glad moment. Thirst-ridden, chilled, and weak as we were, happiness irradiated us. The job was nearly done.

The dawn showed us a storm-torn ocean, and the morning passed without bringing us a sight of the land; but at 1 p.m., through a rift in the flying mists, we got a glimpse of the huge crags of the island and realized that our position had become desperate. We were on a dead lee shore, and we could gauge our approach to the unseen cliffs by the roar of the breakers against the sheer walls of rock. I ordered the double-reefed mainsail to be set in the hope that we might claw off, and this attempt increased the strain upon the boat. The *James Caird* was bumping heavily, and the water was pouring in everywhere. Our thirst was forgotten in the realization of our imminent danger, as we baled unceasingly, and adjusted our weights from time to time; occasional glimpses showed that the shore was nearer. I knew that Annewkow Island lay to the south of us, but our small and badly marked chart showed uncertain reefs in the passage between the island and the mainland, and I dared not trust it, though as a last resort we could try to lie under the lee of the island. The afternoon wore away as we edged down the coast, with the thunder of the breakers in our ears. The approach of evening found us still some distance from Annewkow Island, and, dimly in the twilight, we could see a snow-capped mountain looming above us. The chance of surviving the night, with the driving gale and the implacable sea forcing us on to the lee shore, seemed small. I think most of us had a feeling that the end was very near. Just after 6 p.m., in the dark, as the boat was in the yeasty backwash from the seas flung from this iron-bound coast, then, just when things looked their worst, they changed for the best. I have marvelled often at the thin line that divides success from failure and the sudden turn that leads from apparently certain disaster to comparative safety. The wind suddenly shifted, and we were free once more to make an offing. Almost as soon as the gale eased, the pin that locked the mast to the thwart fell out. It must have been on the point of doing this throughout the hurricane, and if it had gone nothing could have saved us; the mast would have snapped like a carrot. Our backstays had carried away once before when iced up and were not too strongly fastened now. We were thankful indeed for the mercy that had held that pin in its place throughout the hurricane.

We stood off shore again, tired almost to the point of apathy. Our water had long been finished. The last was about a pint of hairy liquid, which we strained through a bit of gauze from the medicine- chest. The pangs of thirst attacked us with redoubled intensity, and I felt that we must make a landing on the following day at almost any hazard. The night wore on. We were very tired. We longed for day. When at last the dawn came on the morning of May 10 there was practically no wind, but a high cross-sea was running.

SOUTH GEORGIA

We made slow progress towards the shore. About 8 a.m. the wind backed to the north-west and threatened another blow. We had sighted in the meantime a big indentation which I thought must be King Haakon Bay, and I decided that we must land there. We set the bows of the boat towards the bay and ran before the freshening gale. Soon we had angry reefs on either side. Great glaciers came down to the sea and offered no landing-place. The sea spouted on the reefs and thundered against the shore. About noon we sighted a line of jagged reef, like blackened teeth, that seemed to bar the entrance to the bay. The entrance was so narrow that we had to take in the oars, and the swell was piling itself right over the reef into the cove; but in a minute or two we were inside, and in the gathering darkness the *James Caird* ran in on a swell and touched the beach. I sprang ashore with the short painter and held on when the boat went out with the backward surge. When the *James Caird* came in again three of the men got ashore, and they held the painter while I climbed some rocks with another line. A slip on the wet rocks twenty feet up nearly closed my part of the story just at the moment when we were achieving safety. A jagged piece of rock held me and at the same time bruised me sorely. However, I made fast the line, and in a few minutes we were all safe on the beach, with the boat floating in the surging water just off the shore. We heard a gurgling sound that was sweet music in our ears, and, peering around, found a stream of fresh water almost at our feet. A moment later we were down on our knees drinking the pure, ice-cold water in long draughts that put new life into us. It was a splendid moment.

The next thing was to get the stores and ballast out of the boat, in order that we might secure her for the night. We carried the stores and gear above high-water mark and threw out the bags of sand and the boulders that we knew so well. Then we attempted to pull the empty boat up the beach, and discovered by this effort how weak we had become. Our united strength was not sufficient to get the *James Caird* clear of the water. Time after time we pulled together, but without avail. I saw that it would be necessary to have food and rest before we beached the boat. We made fast a line to a heavy boulder and set a watch to fend the *James Caird* off the rocks of the beach. Then I sent Crean round to the left side of the cove, about thirty yards away, where I had noticed a little cave as we were running in. He could not see much in the darkness, but reported that the place certainly promised some shelter. We carried the sleeping-bags round and found a mere hollow in the rock-face, with a shingle floor sloping at a steep angle to the sea. There we prepared a hot meal, and when the food was finished I ordered the men to turn in. The time was now about 8 p.m., and I took the first watch beside the *James Caird*, which was still afloat in the tossing water just off the beach.

The final stage of the journey had still to be attempted. I realized that the condition of the party generally, and particularly of McNeish and Vincent, would prevent us putting to sea again except under pressure of dire necessity. The alternative was to attempt the crossing of the island. If we could not get over, then we must try to secure enough food and fuel to keep us alive through the winter, but this possibility was scarcely thinkable. Over on Elephant Island twenty-two men were waiting for the relief that we alone could secure for them. Their plight was worse than ours. We must push on somehow. Several days must elapse before our strength would be sufficiently recovered to allow us to row or sail the last nine miles up to the head of the bay. In the meantime we could make what preparations were possible and dry our clothes by taking advantage of every scrap of heat from the fires we lit for the cooking of our meals. We found that a big hole had been burned in the bottom of Worsley's reindeer sleeping-bag during the night. Worsley had been awakened by a burning sensation in his feet, and had asked the men near him if his bag was all right; they looked and could see nothing wrong. We were all superficially frostbitten about the feet, and this condition caused the extremities to burn painfully, while at the same time sensation was lost in the skin. Worsley thought that the uncomfortable heat of his feet was due to the frost-bites, and he stayed in his bag and presently went to sleep again. He discovered when he turned out in the morning that the tussock-grass which we had laid on the floor of the cave had smouldered outwards from the fire and had actually burned a large hole in the bag beneath his feet. Fortunately, his feet were not harmed.

Our camp, as I have said, lay on the north side of King Haakon Bay near the head. Our path towards the whaling-stations led round the seaward end of the snouted glacier on the east side of the camp and up a snow-slope that appeared to lead to a pass in the great Allardyce Range, which runs north-west and south-east and forms the main backbone of South Georgia. The range dipped opposite the bay into a well-defined pass from east to west. An ice-sheet covered most of the interior, filling the valleys and disguising the configurations of the land, which, indeed, showed only in big rocky ridges, peaks, and nunataks. When we looked up the pass from Peggotty Camp the country to the left appeared to offer two easy paths through to the opposite coast, but we knew that the island was uninhabited at that point (Possession Bay). I planned to climb to the pass and then be guided by the configuration of the country in the selection of a route eastward to Stromness Bay, where the whaling-stations were established in the minor bays, Leith, Husvik, and Stromness.

We overhauled our gear on Thursday, May 18; and hauled our sledge to the lower edge of the snouted glacier. The vehicle proved heavy and cumbrous. We had to lift it empty over bare patches of rock along the shore, and I realized that it would be too heavy for three men to manage amid the snow-plains, glaciers, and peaks of the interior. Worsley and Crean were coming with me, and after consultation we decided to leave the sleeping-bags behind us and make the journey in very light marching order. We would take three days' provisions for each man in the form of sledging ration and biscuit. The food was to be packed in three sacks, so that each member of the party could carry his own supply. Then we were to take the Primus lamp filled with oil, the small cooker, the carpenter's adze (for use as an ice-axe), and the alpine rope, which made a total length of fifty feet when knotted. We might have to lower ourselves down steep slopes or cross crevassed glaciers. The filled lamp would provide six hot meals, which would consist of sledging ration boiled up with biscuit. There were two boxes of matches left, one full and the other partially used. We left the full box with the men at the camp and took the second box, which contained forty-eight matches. I was unfortunate as regarded footgear, since I had given away my heavy Burberry boots on the floe, and had now a comparatively light pair in poor condition. The carpenter assisted me by putting several screws in the sole of each boot with the object of providing a grip on the ice.

McNeish walked about 200 yds with us; he could do no more. Then we said good-bye and he turned back to the camp. The first task was to get round the edge of the snouted glacier, which had points like fingers projecting towards the sea. The waves were reaching the points of these fingers, and we had to rush from one recess to another when the waters receded.

The snow-surface was disappointing. Before, we had been able to move rapidly on hard, packed snow; now we sank over our ankles at each step and progress was slow. After two hours' steady climbing we were 2500 ft. above sea-level. The weather continued fine and calm, and as the ridges drew nearer and the western coast of the island spread out below, the bright moonlight showed us that the interior was broken tremendously. High peaks, impassable cliffs, steep snow-slopes, and sharply descending glaciers were prominent features in all directions, with stretches of snow-plain over laying the ice-sheet of the interior. The slope we were ascending mounted to a ridge and our course lay direct to the top. The moon, which proved a good friend during this journey, threw a long shadow at one point and told us that the surface was broken in our path. Warned in time, we avoided a huge hole capable of swallowing an army. The bay was now about three miles away, and the continued roaring of a big glacier at the head of the bay came to our ears. This glacier, which we had noticed during the stay at Peggotty Camp, seemed to be calving almost continuously.

I had hoped to get a view of the country ahead of us from the top of the slope, but as the surface became more level beneath our feet, a thick fog drifted down. The moon became obscured and produced a diffused light that was more trying than darkness, since it illuminated the fog without guiding our steps. We roped ourselves together as a precaution against holes, crevasses, and precipices, and I broke trail through the soft snow. With almost the full length of the rope between myself and the last man we were able to steer an approximately straight course, since, if I veered to the right or the left when marching into the blank wall of the fog, the last man on the rope could shout a direction. So, like a ship with its "port," "starboard," "steady," we tramped through the fog for the next two hours.

A little later the fog lifted completely, and then we saw that a lake stretched to the horizon, and realized suddenly that we were looking down upon the open sea on the east coast of the island. The slight pulsation at the shore showed that the sea was not even frozen. Evidently we were at the top of Possession Bay, and the island at that point could not be more than five miles across from the head of King Haakon Bay. Our rough chart was inaccurate. There was nothing for it but to start up the glacier again. That was about seven o'clock in the morning, and by nine o'clock we had more than recovered our lost ground. We regained the ridge and then struck south-east, for the chart showed that two more bays indented the coast before Stromness. It was comforting to realize that we would have the eastern water in sight during our journey, although we could see there was no way around the shore line owing to steep cliffs and glaciers.

After passing an area of crevasses we paused for our first meal. We dug a hole in the snow about three feet deep with the adze and put the Primus into it. There was no wind at the moment, but a gust might come suddenly. A hot hoosh was soon eaten and we plodded on towards a sharp ridge between two of the peaks already mentioned. By 11 a.m. we were almost at the crest. The slope had become precipitous and it was necessary to cut steps as we advanced. The adze proved an excellent instrument for this purpose, a blow sufficing to provide a foothold. Anxiously but hopefully I cut the last few steps and stood upon the razor-back, while the other men held the rope and waited for my news. The outlook was disappointing. I looked down a sheer precipice to a chaos of crumpled ice 1500 ft. below. There was no way down for us. The country to the east was a great snow upland, sloping upwards for a distance of seven or eight miles to a height of over 4000 ft. To the north it fell away steeply in glaciers into the bays, and to the south it was broken by huge outfalls from the inland ice-sheet. Our path lay between the glaciers and the outfalls, but first we had to descend from the ridge on which we stood. Cutting steps with the adze, we moved in a lateral direction round the base of a dolomite, which blocked our view to the north. The same precipice confronted us.

It was of the utmost importance for us to get down into the next valley before dark. We were now up 4500 ft. and the night temperature at that elevation would be very low. We had no tent and no sleeping-bags, and our clothes had endured much rough usage and had weathered many storms during the last ten months. In the distance, down the valley below us, we could see tussock-grass close to the shore, and if we could get down it might be possible to dig out a hole in one of the lower snow-banks, line it with dry grass, and make ourselves fairly comfortable for the night. . We could not see the bottom clearly owing to mist and bad light, and the possibility of the slope ending in a sheer fall occurred to us; but the fog that was creeping up behind allowed no time for hesitation. We descended slowly at first, cutting steps in the snow; then the surface became softer, indicating that the gradient was less severe. There could be no turning back now, so we unroped and slid in the fashion of youthful days. When we stopped on a snow-bank at the foot of the slope we found that we had descended at least 900 ft. in two or three minutes. We looked back and saw the grey fingers of the fog appearing on the ridge, as though reaching after the intruders into untrodden wilds. But we had escaped.

At 5 a.m. we were at the foot of the rocky spurs of the range. We were tired, and the wind that blew down from the heights was chilling us. We decided to get down under the lee of a rock for a rest. We put our sticks and the adze on the snow, sat down on them as close to one another as possible, and put our arms round each other. The wind was bringing a little drift with it and the white dust lay on our clothes. I thought that we might be able to keep warm and have half an hour's rest this way. Within a minute my two companions were fast asleep. I realized that it would be disastrous if we all slumbered together, for sleep under such conditions merges into death. After five minutes I shook them into consciousness again, told them that they had slept for half an hour, and gave the word for a fresh start. We were so stiff that for the first two or three hundred yards we marched with our knees bent.

We went through the gap at 6 a.m. with anxious hearts as well as weary bodies. A gentle snow-slope descended at our feet towards a valley that separated our ridge from the hills immediately behind Husvik, and as we stood gazing Worsley said solemnly, "Boss, it looks too good to be true!" Down we went, to be checked presently by the sight of water 2500 ft. below. We could see the little wave-ripples on the black beach, penguins strutting to and fro, and dark objects that looked like seals lolling lazily on the sand. I climbed a ridge above us, cutting steps with the adze, in order to secure an extended view of the country below. At 6.30 a.m. I thought I heard the sound of a steam-whistle. I dared not be certain, but I knew that the men at the whaling-station would be called from their beds about that time. Descending to the camp I told the others, and in intense excitement we watched the chronometer for seven o'clock, when the whalers would be summoned to work. Right to the minute the steam-whistle came to us, borne clearly on the wind across the intervening miles of rock and snow. Never had any one of us heard sweeter music. It was the first sound created by outside human agency that had come to our ears since we left Stromness Bay in December 1914.

So we started away again downwards. We abandoned the Primus lamp, now empty, at the breakfast camp and carried with us one ration and a biscuit each. The deepest snow we had yet encountered clogged our feet, but we plodded downward, and after descending about 500 ft., reducing our altitude to 2000 ft. above sea-level, we thought we saw the way clear ahead. A steep gradient of blue ice was the next obstacle. Worsley and Crean got a firm footing in a hole excavated with the adze and then lowered me as I cut steps until the full 50 ft. of our alpine rope was out. Then I made a hole big enough for the three of us, and the other two men came down the steps. My end of the rope was anchored to the adze and I had settled myself in the hole braced for a strain in case they slipped. When we all stood in the second hole I went down again to make more steps, and in this laborious fashion we spent two hours descending about 500 ft. Halfway down we had to strike away diagonally to the left, for we noticed that the fragments of ice loosened by the adze were taking a leap into space at the bottom of the slope. Eventually we got off the steep ice, very gratefully, at a point where some rocks protruded, and we could see then that there was a perilous precipice directly below the point where we had started to cut steps. A slide down a slippery slope, with the adze and our cooker going ahead, completed this descent, and incidentally did considerable damage to our much-tried trousers.

When we picked ourselves up at the bottom we were not more than 1500 ft. above the sea. A few minutes later we reached the sandy beach. The tracks of some animals were to be seen, and we were puzzled until I remembered that reindeer, brought from Norway, had been placed on the island and now ranged along the lower land of the eastern coast. Our minds were set upon reaching the haunts of man, and at our best speed we went along the beach to another rising ridge of tussock.

At 1.30 p.m. we climbed round a final ridge and saw a little steamer, a whaling-boat, entering the bay 2500 ft, below. A few moments later, as we hurried forward, the masts of a sailing-ship lying at a wharf came in sight. We paused and shook hands, a form of mutual congratulation.

The last lap of the journey proved extraordinarily difficult. Vainly we searched for a safe, or a reasonably safe, way down the steep ice-clad mountain-side. The sole possible pathway seemed to be a channel cut by water running from the upland. Down through icy water we followed the course of this stream. We were wet to the waist, shivering, cold, and tired. Presently our ears detected an unwelcome sound that might have been musical under other conditions. It was the splashing of a waterfall, and we were at the wrong end. When we reached the top of this fall we peered over cautiously and discovered that there was a drop of 25 or 30 ft., with impassable ice-cliffs on both sides. To go up again was scarcely thinkable in our utterly wearied condition. The way down was through the waterfall itself. We made fast one end of our rope to a boulder with some difficulty, due to the fact that the rocks had been worn smooth by the running water. Then Worsley and I lowered Crean, who was the heaviest man. He disappeared altogether in the falling water and came out gasping at the bottom. I went next, sliding down the rope, and Worsley, who was the lightest and most nimble member of the party, came last. At the bottom of the fall we were able to stand again on dry land. The rope could not be recovered. We had flung down the adze from the top of the fall and also the logbook and the cooker wrapped in one of our blouses. That was all, except our wet clothes, that we brought out of the Antarctic, which we had entered a year and a half before with well-found ship, full equipment, and high hopes. That was all of tangible things; but in memories we were rich. We had pierced the veneer of outside things. We had "suffered, starved, and triumphed, grovelled down yet grasped at glory, grown bigger in the bigness of the whole." We had seen God in His splendours, heard the text that Nature renders. We had reached the naked soul of man.

Shivering with cold, yet with hearts light and happy, we set off towards the whaling-station, now not more than a mile and a half distant. The difficulties of the journey lay behind us. We tried to straighten ourselves up a bit, for the thought that there might be women at the station made us painfully conscious of our uncivilized appearance. Our beards were long and our hair was matted. We were unwashed and the garments that we had worn for nearly a year without a change were tattered and stained. Three more unpleasant-looking ruffians could hardly have been imagined. Down we hurried, and when quite close to the station we met two small boys ten or twelve years of age. I asked these lads where the manager's house was situated. They did not answer. They gave us one look—a comprehensive look that did not need to be repeated. Then they ran from us as fast as their legs would carry them. We reached the outskirts of the station and passed through the "digesting-house," which was dark inside. Emerging at the other end, we met an old man, who started as if he had seen the Devil himself and gave us no time to ask any question. He hurried away. This greeting was not friendly. Then we came to the wharf, where the man in charge stuck to his station. I asked him if Mr. Sorlle (the manager) was in the house.

"Who are you?" he asked.

"We have lost our ship and come over the island," I replied.

"You have come over the island?" he said in a tone of entire disbelief.

"My name is Shackleton," I said. "Tell me, when was the war over?"

"The war is not over," he answered. "Millions are being killed. Europe is mad. The world is mad."

TIPS FOR THE TRAIL

First Aid - Nose Bleed

1. Lean forward to keep blood from running down your throat.
2. Pinch your nostrils together for 10 minutes. If it has not stopped bleeding, repeat for another 10 minutes.

TIPS FOR THE TRAIL

First Aid - CPR (Cardiopulmonary Resuscitation)

CPR consists of three main parts, remembered by **ABC**.
A- Airway. Make sure it is open and unobstructed.
B- Breathing. Start rescue breathing if needed.
C- Circulation. Start chest compressions if heart stopped.

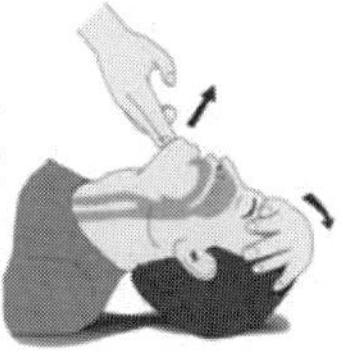

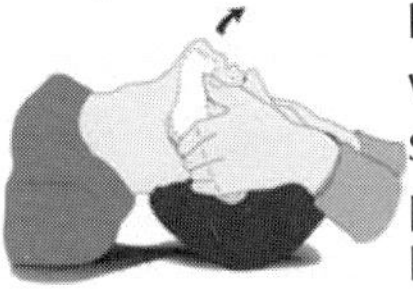

1. Check for victim's breathing. Place them on their back. Open the airway by tilting his chin with one hand and pushing back on the forehead with the other. If you suspect a neck injury, put your fingers behind the jawbone below the ear and push the jaw forward (picture at left).

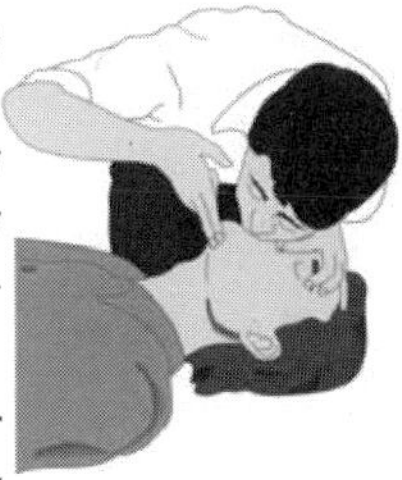

2. Clean out any obstructions in the mouth. Pinch the victim's nostrils, seal his mouth with yours and blow into his mouth. If you have a safety barrier to prevent the spread of disease, you can use that.
3. Repeat every 5 seconds. Check for the chest rising. If air is not getting into the lungs, you may have to recheck for airway obstructions.

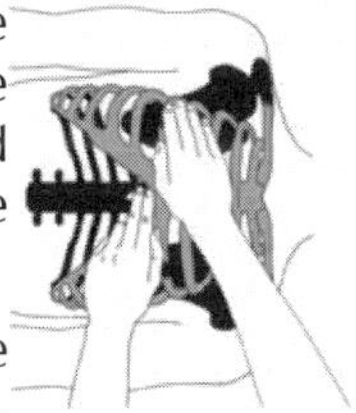

4. If the victim has no pulse, you will have to start chest compressions. Find the end of the sternum and place one hand on the chest two finger widths above this point.
5. Place your other hand on top of the first hand and interlace your fingers.

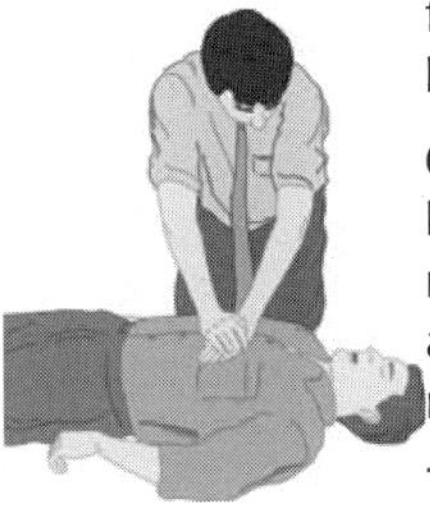

6. Straighten your arms, lock your elbows and position your shoulders directly above your hands. Push down and depress the sternum approximately 1.5 to 2 inches.
7. Do 15 compressions, then inflate the lungs twice. Repeat this sequence four times each minute.

Love of Life
by Jack London

"This out of all will remain -
They have lived and have tossed:
So much of the game will be gain,
Though the gold of the dice has been lost."

They limped painfully down the bank, and once the foremost of the two men staggered among the rough-strewn rocks. They were tired and weak, and their faces had the drawn expression of patience which comes of hardship long endured. They were heavily burdened with blanket packs which were strapped to their shoulders. Head-straps, passing across the forehead, helped support these packs. Each man carried a rifle. They walked in a stooped posture, the shoulders well forward, the head still farther forward, the eyes bent upon the ground.

"I wish we had just about two of them cartridges that's layin' in that cache of ourn," said the second man.

His voice was utterly and drearily expressionless. He spoke without enthusiasm; and the first man, limping into the milky stream that foamed over the rocks, vouchsafed no reply.

The other man followed at his heels. They did not remove their foot-gear, though the water was icy cold—so cold that their ankles ached and their feet went numb. In places the water dashed against their knees, and both men staggered for footing.

The man who followed slipped on a smooth boulder, nearly fell, but recovered himself with a violent effort, at the same time uttering a sharp exclamation of pain. He seemed faint and dizzy and put out his free hand while he reeled, as though seeking support against the air. When he had steadied himself he stepped forward, but reeled again and nearly fell. Then he stood still and looked at the other man, who had never turned his head.

The man stood still for fully a minute, as though debating with himself. Then he called out:

"I say, Bill, I've sprained my ankle."

Bill staggered on through the milky water. He did not look around. The man watched him go, and though his face was expressionless as ever, his eyes were like the eyes of a wounded deer.

The other man limped up the farther bank and continued straight on without looking back. The man in the stream watched him. His lips trembled a little, so that the rough thatch of brown hair which covered them was visibly agitated. His tongue even strayed out to moisten them.

"Bill!" he cried out.

It was the pleading cry of a strong man in distress, but Bill's head did not turn. The man watched him go, limping grotesquely and lurching forward with stammering gait up the slow slope toward the soft sky-line of the low-lying hill. He watched him go till he passed over the crest and disappeared. Then he turned his gaze and slowly took in the circle of the world that remained to him now that Bill was gone.

Near the horizon the sun was smouldering dimly, almost obscured by formless mists and vapors, which gave an impression of mass and density without outline or tangibility. The man pulled out his watch, the while resting his weight on one leg. It was four o'clock, and as the season was near the last of July or first of August,—he did not know the precise date within a week or two,—he knew that the sun roughly marked the northwest. He looked to the south and knew that somewhere beyond those bleak hills lay the Great Bear Lake; also, he knew that in that direction the Arctic Circle cut its forbidding way across the Canadian Barrens. This stream in which he stood was a feeder to the Coppermine River, which in turn flowed north and emptied into Coronation Gulf and the Arctic Ocean. He had never been there, but he had seen it, once, on a Hudson Bay Company chart.

Again his gaze completed the circle of the world about him. It was not a heartening spectacle. Everywhere was soft sky-line. The hills were all low-lying. There were no trees, no shrubs, no grasses—naught but a tremendous and terrible desolation that sent fear swiftly dawning into his eyes.

"Bill!" he whispered, once and twice; "Bill!"

He cowered in the midst of the milky water, as though the vastness were pressing in upon him with overwhelming force, brutally crushing him with its complacent awfulness. He began to shake as with an ague-fit, till the gun fell from his hand with a splash. This served to rouse him. He fought with his fear and pulled himself together, groping in the water and recovering the weapon. He hitched his pack farther over on his left shoulder, so as to take a portion of its weight from off the injured ankle. Then he proceeded, slowly and carefully, wincing with pain, to the bank.

He did not stop. With a desperation that was madness, unmindful of the pain, he hurried up the slope to the crest of the hill over which his comrade had disappeared—more grotesque and comical by far than that limping, jerking comrade. But at the crest he saw a shallow valley, empty of life. He fought with his fear again, overcame it, hitched the pack still farther over on his left shoulder, and lurched on down the slope.

The bottom of the valley was soggy with water, which the thick moss held, spongelike, close to the surface. This water squirted out from under his feet at every step, and each time he lifted a foot the action culminated in a sucking sound as the wet moss reluctantly released its grip. He picked his way from muskeg to muskeg, and followed the other man's footsteps along and across the rocky ledges which thrust like islets through the sea of moss.

Though alone, he was not lost. Farther on he knew he would come to where dead spruce and fir, very small and weazened, bordered the shore of a little lake, the Titchin-Nichilie, in the tongue of the country, the "land of little sticks." And into that lake flowed a small stream, the water of which was not milky. There was rush-grass on that stream—this he remembered well—but no timber, and he would follow it till its first trickle ceased at a divide. He would cross this divide to the first trickle of another stream, flowing to the west, which he would follow until it emptied into the river Dease, and here he would find a cache under an upturned canoe and piled over with many rocks. And in this cache would be ammunition for his empty gun, fish-hooks and lines, a small net—all the utilities for the killing and snaring of food. Also, he would find flour,—not much,—a piece of bacon, and some beans.

Bill would be waiting for him there, and they would paddle away south down the Dease to the Great Bear Lake. And south across the lake they would go, ever south, till they gained the Mackenzie. And south, still south, they would go, while the winter raced vainly after them, and the ice formed in the eddies, and the days grew chill and crisp, south to some warm Hudson Bay Company post, where timber grew tall and generous and there was grub without end.

These were the thoughts of the man as he strove onward. But hard as he strove with his body, he strove equally hard with his mind, trying to think that Bill had not deserted him, that Bill would surely wait for him at the cache. He was compelled to think this thought, or else there would not be any use to strive, and he would have lain down and died. And as the dim ball of the sun sank slowly into the northwest he covered every inch—and many times—of his and Bill's flight south before the downcoming winter. And he conned the grub of the cache and the grub of the Hudson Bay Company post over and over again. He had not eaten for two days; for a far longer time he had not had all he wanted to eat. Often he stooped and picked pale muskeg berries, put them into his mouth, and chewed and swallowed them. A muskeg berry is a bit of seed enclosed in a bit of water. In the mouth the water melts away and the seed chews sharp and bitter. The man knew there was no nourishment in the berries, but he chewed them patiently with a hope greater than knowledge and defying experience.

At nine o'clock he stubbed his toe on a rocky ledge, and from sheer weariness and weakness staggered and fell. He lay for some time, without movement, on his side. Then he slipped out of the pack-straps and clumsily dragged himself into a sitting posture. It was not yet dark, and in the lingering twilight he groped about among the rocks for shreds of dry moss. When he had gathered a heap he built a fire,—a smouldering, smudgy fire,—and put a tin pot of water on to boil.

He unwrapped his pack and the first thing he did was to count his matches. There were sixty-seven. He counted them three times to make sure. He divided them into several portions, wrapping them in oil paper, disposing of one bunch in his empty tobacco pouch, of another bunch in the inside band of his battered hat, of a third bunch under his shirt on the chest. This accomplished, a panic came upon him, and he unwrapped them all and counted them again. There were still sixty-seven.

He dried his wet foot-gear by the fire. The moccasins were in soggy shreds. The blanket socks were worn through in places, and his feet were raw and bleeding. His ankle was throbbing, and he gave it an examination. It had swollen to the size of his knee. He tore a long strip from one of his two blankets and bound the ankle tightly. He tore other strips and bound them about his feet to serve for both moccasins and socks. Then he drank the pot of water, steaming hot, wound his watch, and crawled between his blankets.

He slept like a dead man. The brief darkness around midnight came and went. The sun arose in the northeast—at least the day dawned in that quarter, for the sun was hidden by gray clouds.

At six o'clock he awoke, quietly lying on his back. He gazed straight up into the gray sky and knew that he was hungry. As he rolled over on his elbow he was startled by a loud snort, and saw a bull caribou regarding him with alert curiosity. The animal was not mere than fifty feet away, and instantly into the man's mind leaped the vision and the savor of a caribou steak sizzling and frying over a fire. Mechanically he reached for the empty gun, drew a bead, and pulled the trigger. The bull snorted and leaped away, his hoofs rattling and clattering as he fled across the ledges.

The man cursed and flung the empty gun from him. He groaned aloud as he started to drag himself to his feet. It was a slow and arduous task.

His joints were like rusty hinges. They worked harshly in their sockets, with much friction, and each bending or unbending was accomplished only through a sheer exertion of will. When he finally gained his feet, another minute or so was consumed in straightening up, so that he could stand erect as a man should stand.

He crawled up a small knoll and surveyed the prospect. There were no trees, no bushes, nothing but a gray sea of moss scarcely diversified by gray rocks, gray lakelets, and gray streamlets. The sky was gray. There was no sun nor hint of sun. He had no idea of north, and he had forgotten the way he had come to this spot the night before. But he was not lost. He knew that. Soon he would come to the land of the little sticks. He felt that it lay off to the left somewhere, not far—possibly just over the next low hill.

He went back to put his pack into shape for travelling. He assured himself of the existence of his three separate parcels of matches, though he did not stop to count them. But he did linger, debating, over a squat moose-hide sack. It was not large. He could hide it under his two hands. He knew that it weighed fifteen pounds,—as much as all the rest of the pack,—and it worried him. He finally set it to one side and proceeded to roll the pack. He paused to gaze at the squat moose-hide sack. He picked it up hastily with a defiant glance about him, as though the desolation were trying to rob him of it; and when he rose to his feet to stagger on into the day, it was included in the pack on his back.

He bore away to the left, stopping now and again to eat muskeg berries. His ankle had stiffened, his limp was more pronounced, but the pain of it was as nothing compared with the pain of his stomach. The hunger pangs were sharp. They gnawed and gnawed until he could not keep his mind steady on the course he must pursue to gain the land of little sticks. The muskeg berries did not allay this gnawing, while they made his tongue and the roof of his mouth sore with their irritating bite.

He came upon a valley where rock ptarmigan rose on whirring wings from the ledges and muskegs. Ker—ker—ker was the cry they made. He threw stones at them, but could not hit them. He placed his pack on the ground and stalked them as a cat stalks a sparrow. The sharp rocks cut through his pants' legs till his knees left a trail of blood; but the hurt was lost in the hurt of his hunger. He squirmed over the wet moss, saturating his clothes and chilling his body; but he was not aware of it, so great was his fever for food. And always the ptarmigan rose, whirring, before him, till their ker—ker—ker became a mock to him, and he cursed them and cried aloud at them with their own cry.

Once he crawled upon one that must have been asleep. He did not see it till it shot up in his face from its rocky nook. He made a clutch as startled as was the rise of the ptarmigan, and there remained in his hand three tail-feathers. As he watched its flight he hated it, as though it had done him some terrible wrong. Then he returned and shouldered his pack.

As the day wore along he came into valleys or swales where game was more plentiful. A band of caribou passed by, twenty and odd animals, tantalizingly within rifle range. He felt a wild desire to run after them, a certitude that he could run them down. A black fox came toward him, carrying a ptarmigan in his mouth. The man shouted. It was a fearful cry, but the fox, leaping away in fright, did not drop the ptarmigan.

Late in the afternoon he followed a stream, milky with lime, which ran through sparse patches of rush-grass. Grasping these rushes firmly near the root, he pulled up what resembled a young onion- sprout no larger than a shingle-nail. It was tender, and his teeth sank into it with a crunch that promised deliciously of food. But its fibers were tough. It was composed of stringy filaments saturated with water, like the berries, and devoid of nourishment. He threw off his pack and went into the rush-grass on hands and knees, crunching and munching, like some bovine creature.

He was very weary and often wished to rest—to lie down and sleep; but he was continually driven on—not so much by his desire to gain the land of little sticks as by his hunger. He searched little ponds for frogs and dug up the earth with his nails for worms, though he knew in spite that neither frogs nor worms existed so far north.

He looked into every pool of water vainly, until, as the long twilight came on, he discovered a solitary fish, the size of a minnow, in such a pool. He plunged his arm in up to the shoulder, but it eluded him. He reached for it with both hands and stirred up the milky mud at the bottom. In his excitement he fell in, wetting himself to the waist. Then the water was too muddy to admit of his seeing the fish, and he was compelled to wait until the sediment had settled.

The pursuit was renewed, till the water was again muddied. But he could not wait. He unstrapped the tin bucket and began to bale the pool. He baled wildly at first, splashing himself and flinging the water so short a distance that it ran back into the pool. He worked more carefully, striving to be cool, though his heart was pounding against his chest and his hands were trembling. At the end of half an hour the pool was nearly dry. Not a cupful of water remained. And there was no fish. He found a hidden crevice among the stones through which it had escaped to the adjoining and larger pool—a pool which he could not empty in a night and a day. Had he known of the crevice, he could have closed it with a rock at the beginning and the fish would have been his.

Thus he thought, and crumpled up and sank down upon the wet earth. At first he cried softly to himself, then he cried loudly to the pitiless desolation that ringed him around; and for a long time after he was shaken by great dry sobs.

He built a fire and warmed himself by drinking quarts of hot water, and made camp on a rocky ledge in the same fashion he had the night before. The last thing he did was to see that his matches were dry and to wind his watch. The blankets were wet and clammy. His ankle pulsed with pain. But he knew only that he was hungry, and through his restless sleep he dreamed of feasts and banquets and of food served and spread in all imaginable ways.

He awoke chilled and sick. There was no sun. The gray of earth and sky had become deeper, more profound. A raw wind was blowing, and the first flurries of snow were whitening the hilltops. The air about him thickened and grew white while he made a fire and boiled more water. It was wet snow, half rain, and the flakes were large and soggy. At first they melted as soon as they came in contact with the earth, but ever more fell, covering the ground, putting out the fire, spoiling his supply of moss-fuel.

This was a signal for him to strap on his pack and stumble onward, he knew not where. He was not concerned with the land of little sticks, nor with Bill and the cache under the upturned canoe by the river Dease. He was mastered by the verb "to eat." He was hunger-mad. He took no heed of the course he pursued, so long as that course led him through the swale bottoms. He felt his way through the wet snow to the watery muskeg berries, and went by feel as he pulled up the rush-grass by the roots. But it was tasteless stuff and did not satisfy. He found a weed that tasted sour and he ate all he could find of it, which was not much, for it was a creeping growth, easily hidden under the several inches of snow.

He had no fire that night, nor hot water, and crawled under his blanket to sleep the broken hunger-sleep. The snow turned into a cold rain. He awakened many times to feel it falling on his upturned face. Day came—a gray day and no sun. It had ceased raining. Thc keenness of his hunger had departed. Sensibility, as far as concerned the yearning for food, had been exhausted. There was a dull, heavy ache in his stomach, but it did not bother him so much. He was more rational, and once more he was chiefly interested in the land of little sticks and the cache by the river Dease.

He ripped the remnant of one of his blankets into strips and bound his bleeding feet. Also, he recinched the injured ankle and prepared himself for a day of travel. When he came to his pack, he paused long over the squat moose-hide sack, but in the end it went with him.

The snow had melted under the rain, and only the hilltops showed white. The sun came out, and he succeeded in locating the points of the compass, though he knew now that he was lost. Perhaps, in his previous days' wanderings, he had edged away too far to the left. He now bore off to the right to counteract the possible deviation from his true course.

Though the hunger pangs were no longer so exquisite, he realized that he was weak. He was compelled to pause for frequent rests, when he attacked the muskeg berries and rush-grass patches. His tongue felt dry and large, as though covered with a fine hairy growth, and it tasted bitter in his mouth. His heart gave him a great deal of trouble. When he had travelled a few minutes it would begin a remorseless thump, thump, thump, and then leap up and away in a painful flutter of beats that choked him and made him go faint and dizzy.

In the middle of the day he found two minnows in a large pool. It was impossible to bale it, but he was calmer now and managed to catch them in his tin bucket. They were no longer than his little finger, but he was not particularly hungry. The dull ache in his stomach had been growing duller and fainter. It seemed almost that his stomach was dozing. He ate the fish raw, masticating with painstaking care, for the eating was an act of pure reason. While he had no desire to eat, he knew that he must eat to live.

In the evening he caught three more minnows, eating two and saving the third for breakfast. The sun had dried stray shreds of moss, and he was able to warm himself with hot water. He had not covered more than ten miles that day; and the next day, travelling whenever his heart permitted him, he covered no more than five miles. But his stomach did not give him the slightest uneasiness. It had gone to sleep. He was in a strange country, too, and the caribou were growing more plentiful, also the wolves. Often their yelps drifted across the desolation, and once he saw three of them slinking away before his path.

Another night; and in the morning, being more rational, he untied the leather string that fastened the squat moose-hide sack. From its open mouth poured a yellow stream of coarse gold-dust and nuggets. He roughly divided the gold in halves, caching one half on a prominent ledge, wrapped in a piece of blanket, and returning the other half to the sack. He also began to use strips of the one remaining blanket for his feet. He still clung to his gun, for there were cartridges in that cache by the river Dease.

This was a day of fog, and this day hunger awoke in him again. He was very weak and was afflicted with a giddiness which at times blinded him. It was no uncommon thing now for him to stumble and fall; and stumbling once, he fell squarely into a ptarmigan nest. There were four newly hatched chicks, a day old—little specks of pulsating life no more than a mouthful; and he ate them ravenously, thrusting them alive into his mouth and crunching them like egg-shells between his teeth. The mother ptarmigan beat about him with great outcry. He used his gun as a club with which to knock her over, but she dodged out of reach. He threw stones at her and with one chance shot broke a wing. Then she fluttered away, running, trailing the broken wing, with him in pursuit.

The little chicks had no more than whetted his appetite. He hopped and bobbed clumsily along on his injured ankle, throwing stones and screaming hoarsely at times; at other times hopping and bobbing silently along, picking himself up grimly and patiently when he fell, or rubbing his eyes with his hand when the giddiness threatened to overpower him.

The chase led him across swampy ground in the bottom of the valley, and he came upon footprints in the soggy moss. They were not his own—he could see that. They must be Bill's. But he could not stop, for the mother ptarmigan was running on. He would catch her first, then he would return and investigate.

He exhausted the mother ptarmigan; but he exhausted himself. She lay panting on her side. He lay panting on his side, a dozen feet away, unable to crawl to her. And as he recovered she recovered, fluttering out of reach as his hungry hand went out to her. The chase was resumed. Night settled down and she escaped. He stumbled from weakness and pitched head foremost on his face, cutting his cheek, his pack upon his back. He did not move for a long while; then he rolled over on his side, wound his watch, and lay there until morning.

Another day of fog. Half of his last blanket had gone into foot-wrappings. He failed to pick up Bill's trail. It did not matter. His hunger was driving him too compellingly—only—only he wondered if Bill, too, were lost. By midday the irk of his pack became too oppressive. Again he divided the gold, this time merely spilling half of it on the ground. In the afternoon he threw the rest of it away, there remaining to him only the half-blanket, the tin bucket, and the rifle.

An hallucination began to trouble him. He felt confident that one cartridge remained to him. It was in the chamber of the rifle and he had overlooked it. On the other hand, he knew all the time that the chamber was empty. But the hallucination persisted. He fought it off for hours, then threw his rifle open and was confronted with emptiness. The disappointment was as bitter as though he had really expected to find the cartridge.

He plodded on for half an hour, when the hallucination arose again. Again he fought it, and still it persisted, till for very relief he opened his rifle to unconvince himself. At times his mind wandered farther afield, and he plodded on, a mere automaton, strange conceits and whimsicalities gnawing at his brain like worms. But these excursions out of the real were of brief duration, for ever the pangs of the hunger-bite called him back. He was jerked back abruptly once from such an excursion by a sight that caused him nearly to faint. He reeled and swayed, doddering like a drunken man to keep from falling. Before him stood a horse. A horse! He could not believe his eyes. A thick mist was in them, intershot with sparkling points of light. He rubbed his eyes savagely to clear his vision, and beheld, not a horse, but a great brown bear. The animal was studying him with bellicose curiosity.

The man had brought his gun halfway to his shoulder before he realized. He lowered it and drew his hunting-knife from its beaded sheath at his hip. Before him was meat and life. He ran his thumb along the edge of his knife. It was sharp. The point was sharp. He would fling himself upon the bear and kill it. But his heart began its warning thump, thump, thump. Then followed the wild upward leap and tattoo of flutters, the pressing as of an iron band about his forehead, the creeping of the dizziness into his brain.

His desperate courage was evicted by a great surge of fear. In his weakness, what if the animal attacked him? He drew himself up to his most imposing stature, gripping the knife and staring hard at the bear. The bear advanced clumsily a couple of steps, reared up, and gave vent to a tentative growl. If the man ran, he would run after him; but the man did not run. He was animated now with the courage of fear. He, too, growled, savagely, terribly, voicing the fear that is to life germane and that lies twisted about life's deepest roots.

The bear edged away to one side, growling menacingly, himself appalled by this mysterious creature that appeared upright and unafraid. But the man did not move. He stood like a statue till the danger was past, when he yielded to a fit of trembling and sank down into the wet moss.

He pulled himself together and went on, afraid now in a new way. It was not the fear that he should die passively from lack of food, but that he should be destroyed violently before starvation had exhausted the last particle of the endeavor in him that made toward surviving. There were the wolves. Back and forth across the desolation drifted their howls, weaving the very air into a fabric of menace that was so tangible that he found himself, arms in the air, pressing it back from him as it might be the walls of a wind-blown tent.

Now and again the wolves, in packs of two and three, crossed his path. But they steered clear of him. They were not in sufficient numbers, and besides they were hunting the caribou, which did not battle, while this strange creature that walked erect might scratch and bite.

In the late afternoon he came upon scattered bones where the wolves had made a kill. The debris had been a caribou calf an hour before, squawking and running and very much alive. He contemplated the bones, clean-picked and polished, pink with the cell-life in them which had not yet died. Could it possibly be that he might be that ere the day was done! Such was life, eh? A vain and fleeting thing. It was only life that pained. There was no hurt in death. To die was to sleep. It meant cessation, rest. Then why was he not content to die?

But he did not moralize long. He was squatting in the moss, a bone in his mouth, sucking at the shreds of life that still dyed it faintly pink. The sweet meaty taste, thin and elusive almost as a memory, maddened him. He closed his jaws on the bones and crunched. Sometimes it was the bone that broke, sometimes his teeth. Then he crushed the bones between rocks, pounded them to a pulp, and swallowed them. He pounded his fingers, too, in his haste, and yet found a moment in which to feel surprise at the fact that his fingers did not hurt much when caught under the descending rock.

Came frightful days of snow and rain. He did not know when he made camp, when he broke camp. He travelled in the night as much as in the day. He rested wherever he fell, crawled on whenever the dying life in him flickered up and burned less dimly. He, as a man, no longer strove. It was the life in him, unwilling to die, that drove him on. He did not suffer. His nerves had become blunted, numb, while his mind was filled with weird visions and delicious dreams.

But ever he sucked and chewed on the crushed bones of the caribou calf, the least remnants of which he had gathered up and carried with him. He crossed no more hills or divides, but automatically followed a large stream which flowed through a wide and shallow valley. He did not see this stream nor this valley. He saw nothing save visions. Soul and body walked or crawled side by side, yet apart, so slender was the thread that bound them.

He awoke in his right mind, lying on his back on a rocky ledge. The sun was shining bright and warm. Afar off he heard the squawking of caribou calves. He was aware of vague memories of rain and wind and snow, but whether he had been beaten by the storm for two days or two weeks he did not know.

For some time he lay without movement, the genial sunshine pouring upon him and saturating his miserable body with its warmth. A fine day, he thought. Perhaps he could manage to locate himself. By a painful effort he rolled over on his side. Below him flowed a wide and sluggish river. Its unfamiliarity puzzled him. Slowly he followed it with his eyes, winding in wide sweeps among the bleak, bare hills, bleaker and barer and lower-lying than any hills he had yet encountered. Slowly, deliberately, without excitement or more than the most casual interest, he followed the course of the strange stream toward the sky-line and saw it emptying into a bright and shining sea. He was still unexcited. Most unusual, he thought, a vision or a mirage—more likely a vision, a trick of his disordered mind. He was confirmed in this by sight of a ship lying at anchor in the midst of the shining sea. He closed his eyes for a while, then opened them. Strange how the vision persisted! Yet not strange. He knew there were no seas or ships in the heart of the barren lands, just as he had known there was no cartridge in the empty rifle.

He heard a snuffle behind him—a half-choking gasp or cough. Very slowly, because of his exceeding weakness and stiffness, he rolled over on his other side. He could see nothing near at hand, but he waited patiently. Again came the snuffle and cough, and outlined between two jagged rocks not a score of feet away he made out the gray head of a wolf. The sharp ears were not pricked so sharply as he had seen them on other wolves; the eyes were bleared and bloodshot, the head seemed to droop limply and forlornly. The animal blinked continually in the sunshine. It seemed sick. As he looked it snuffled and coughed again.

This, at least, was real, he thought, and turned on the other side so that he might see the reality of the world which had been veiled from him before by the vision. But the sea still shone in the distance and the ship was plainly discernible. Was it reality, after all? He closed his eyes for a long while and thought, and then it came to him. He had been making north by east, away from the Dease Divide and into the Coppermine Valley. This wide and sluggish river was the Coppermine. That shining sea was the Arctic Ocean. That ship was a whaler, strayed east, far east, from the mouth of the Mackenzie, and it was lying at anchor in Coronation Gulf. He remembered the Hudson Bay Company chart he had seen long ago, and it was all clear and reasonable to him.

He sat up and turned his attention to immediate affairs. He had worn through the blanket-wrappings, and his feet were shapeless lumps of raw meat. His last blanket was gone. Rifle and knife were both missing. He had lost his hat somewhere, with the bunch of matches in the band, but the matches against his chest were safe and dry inside the tobacco pouch and oil paper. He looked at his watch. It marked eleven o'clock and was still running. Evidently he had kept it wound.

He was calm and collected. Though extremely weak, he had no sensation of pain. He was not hungry. The thought of food was not even pleasant to him, and whatever he did was done by his reason alone. He ripped off his pants' legs to the knees and bound them about his feet. Somehow he had succeeded in retaining the tin bucket. He would have some hot water before he began what he foresaw was to be a terrible journey to the ship.

His movements were slow. He shook as with a palsy. When he started to collect dry moss, he found he could not rise to his feet. He tried again and again, then contented himself with crawling about on hands and knees. Once he crawled near to the sick wolf. The animal dragged itself reluctantly out of his way, licking its chops with a tongue which seemed hardly to have the strength to curl. The man noticed that the tongue was not the customary healthy red. It was a yellowish brown and seemed coated with a rough and half-dry mucus.

After he had drunk a quart of hot water the man found he was able to stand, and even to walk as well as a dying man might be supposed to walk. Every minute or so he was compelled to rest. His steps were feeble and uncertain, just as the wolf's that trailed him were feeble and uncertain; and that night, when the shining sea was blotted out by blackness, he knew he was nearer to it by no more than four miles.

Throughout the night he heard the cough of the sick wolf, and now and then the squawking of the caribou calves. There was life all around him, but it was strong life, very much alive and well, and he knew the sick wolf clung to the sick man's trail in the hope that the man would die first. In the morning, on opening his eyes, he beheld it regarding him with a wistful and hungry stare. It stood crouched, with tail between its legs, like a miserable and woe-begone dog. It shivered in the chill morning wind, and grinned dispiritedly when the man spoke to it in a voice that achieved no more than a hoarse whisper.

The sun rose brightly, and all morning the man tottered and fell toward the ship on the shining sea. The weather was perfect. It was the brief Indian Summer of the high latitudes. It might last a week. To-morrow or next day it might he gone.

In the afternoon the man came upon a trail. It was of another man, who did not walk, but who dragged himself on all fours. The man thought it might be Bill, but he thought in a dull, uninterested way. He had no curiosity. In fact, sensation and emotion had left him. He was no longer susceptible to pain. Stomach and nerves had gone to sleep. Yet the life that was in him drove him on. He was very weary, but it refused to die. It was because it refused to die that he still ate muskeg berries and minnows, drank his hot water, and kept a wary eye on the sick wolf.

He followed the trail of the other man who dragged himself along, and soon came to the end of it—a few fresh-picked bones where the soggy moss was marked by the foot-pads of many wolves. He saw a squat moose-hide sack, mate to his own, which had been torn by sharp teeth. He picked it up, though its weight was almost too much for his feeble fingers. Bill had carried it to the last. Ha! ha! He would have the laugh on Bill. He would survive and carry it to the ship in the shining sea. His mirth was hoarse and ghastly, like a raven's croak, and the sick wolf joined him, howling lugubriously. The man ceased suddenly. How could he have the laugh on Bill if that were Bill; if those bones, so pinky-white and clean, were Bill?

He turned away. Well, Bill had deserted him; but he would not take the gold, nor would he suck Bill's bones. Bill would have, though, had it been the other way around, he mused as he staggered on.

He came to a pool of water. Stooping over in quest of minnows, he jerked his head back as though he had been stung. He had caught sight of his reflected face. So horrible was it that sensibility awoke long enough to be shocked. There were three minnows in the pool, which was too large to drain; and after several ineffectual attempts to catch them in the tin bucket he forbore. He was afraid, because of his great weakness, that he might fall in and drown. It was for this reason that he did not trust himself to the river astride one of the many drift-logs which lined its sand-spits.

That day he decreased the distance between him and the ship by three miles; the next day by two—for he was crawling now as Bill had crawled; and the end of the fifth day found the ship still seven miles away and him unable to make even a mile a day. Still the Indian Summer held on, and he continued to crawl and faint, turn and turn about; and ever the sick wolf coughed and wheezed at his heels. His knees had become raw meat like his feet, and though he padded them with the shirt from his back it was a red track he left behind him on the moss and stones. Once, glancing back, he saw the wolf licking hungrily his bleeding trail, and he saw sharply what his own end might be—unless—unless he could get the wolf. Then began as grim a tragedy of existence as was ever played—a sick man that crawled, a sick wolf that limped, two creatures dragging their dying carcasses across the desolation and hunting each other's lives.

Had it been a well wolf, it would not have mattered so much to the man; but the thought of going to feed the maw of that loathsome and all but dead thing was repugnant to him. He was finicky. His mind had begun to wander again, and to be perplexed by hallucinations, while his lucid intervals grew rarer and shorter.

He was awakened once from a faint by a wheeze close in his ear. The wolf leaped lamely back, losing its footing and falling in its weakness. It was ludicrous, but he was not amused. Nor was he even afraid. He was too far gone for that. But his mind was for the moment clear, and he lay and considered. The ship was no more than four miles away. He could see it quite distinctly when he rubbed the mists out of his eyes, and he could see the white sail of a small boat cutting the water of the shining sea. But he could never crawl those four miles. He knew that, and was very calm in the knowledge. He knew that he could not crawl half a mile. And yet he wanted to live. It was unreasonable that he should die after all he had undergone. Fate asked too much of him. And, dying, he declined to die. It was stark madness, perhaps, but in the very grip of Death he defied Death and refused to die.

He closed his eyes and composed himself with infinite precaution. He steeled himself to keep above the suffocating languor that lapped like a rising tide through all the wells of his being. It was very like a sea, this deadly languor, that rose and rose and drowned his consciousness bit by bit. Sometimes he was all but submerged, swimming through oblivion with a faltering stroke; and again, by some strange alchemy of soul, he would find another shred of will and strike out more strongly.

Without movement he lay on his back, and he could hear, slowly drawing near and nearer, the wheezing intake and output of the sick wolf's breath. It drew closer, ever closer, through an infinitude of time, and he did not move. It was at his ear. The harsh dry tongue grated like sandpaper against his cheek. His hands shot out—or at least he willed them to shoot out. The fingers were curved like talons, but they closed on empty air. Swiftness and certitude require strength, and the man had not this strength.

The patience of the wolf was terrible. The man's patience was no less terrible. For half a day he lay motionless, fighting off unconsciousness and waiting for the thing that was to feed upon him and upon which he wished to feed. Sometimes the languid sea rose over him and he dreamed long dreams; but ever through it all, waking and dreaming, he waited for the wheezing breath and the harsh caress of the tongue.

He did not hear the breath, and he slipped slowly from some dream to the feel of the tongue along his hand. He waited. The fangs pressed softly; the pressure increased; the wolf was exerting its last strength in an effort to sink teeth in the food for which it had waited so long. But the man had waited long, and the lacerated hand closed on the jaw. Slowly, while the wolf struggled feebly and the hand clutched feebly, the other hand crept across to a grip. Five minutes later the whole weight of the man's body was on top of the wolf. The hands had not sufficient strength to choke the wolf, but the face of the man was pressed close to the throat of the wolf and the mouth of the man was full of hair. At the end of half an hour the man was aware of a warm trickle in his throat. It was not pleasant. It was like molten lead being forced into his stomach, and it was forced by his will alone. Later the man rolled over on his back and slept.

There were some members of a scientific expedition on the whale-ship *Bedford*. From the deck they remarked a strange object on the shore. It was moving down the beach toward the water. They were unable to classify it, and, being scientific men, they climbed into the whale-boat alongside and went ashore to see. And they saw something that was alive but which could hardly be called a man. It was blind, unconscious. It squirmed along the ground like some monstrous worm. Most of its efforts were ineffectual, but it was persistent, and it writhed and twisted and went ahead perhaps a score of feet an hour.

Three weeks afterward the man lay in a bunk on the whale-ship *Bedford*, and with tears streaming down his wasted cheeks told who he was and what he had undergone. He also babbled incoherently of his mother, of sunny Southern California, and a home among the orange groves and flowers.

The days were not many after that when he sat at table with the scientific men and ship's officers. He gloated over the spectacle of so much food, watching it anxiously as it went into the mouths of others. With the disappearance of each mouthful an expression of deep regret came into his eyes. He was quite sane, yet he hated those men at mealtime. He was haunted by a fear that the food would not last. He inquired of the cook, the cabin-boy, the captain, concerning the food stores. They reassured him countless times; but he could not believe them, and pried cunningly about the lazarette to see with his own eyes.

It was noticed that the man was getting fat. He grew stouter with each day. The scientific men shook their heads and theorized. They limited the man at his meals, but still his girth increased and he swelled prodigiously under his shirt.

The sailors grinned. They knew. And when the scientific men set a watch on the man, they knew too. They saw him slouch for'ard after breakfast, and, like a mendicant, with outstretched palm, accost a sailor. The sailor grinned and passed him a fragment of sea biscuit. He clutched it avariciously, looked at it as a miser looks at gold, and thrust it into his shirt bosom. Similar were the donations from other grinning sailors.

The scientific men were discreet. They let him alone. But they privily examined his bunk. It was lined with hardtack; the mattress was stuffed with hardtack; every nook and cranny was filled with hardtack. Yet he was sane. He was taking precautions against another possible famine—that was all. He would recover from it, the scientific men said; and he did, ere the *Bedford's* anchor rumbled down in San Francisco Bay.

TIPS FOR THE TRAIL

What to Do...When Caught by Lightning

Try to Avoid the Storm

- Lightning may strike ahead of the storm. To determine how far away the lightning is, count the time between seeing the bolt and hearing the sound and divide by 5. Sound travels one mile in approximately 5 seconds. If it takes 10 seconds for the sound to reach you, the lightning is 2 miles away.
- The summits of mountains, crests of ridges, slopes above timberline, and large meadows are extremely hazardous places to be during lightning storms. If you are caught in such an exposed place, quickly descend to a lower elevation, away from the direction of the approaching storm,.
- If on open water, get off the water and out of the boat.
- If you are in a car, stay in the car and avoid touching metal.
- A dense forest located in a depression provides the best protection. Avoid taking shelter under isolated trees or trees much taller than adjacent trees. Stay away from water, metal objects, and other substances that will conduct electricity long distances.

When the lightning approaches

- Place metal objects (packs, poles, etc.) away from you.
- Sit on an insulated pad or your sleeping bag. Squat down and keep your head low. You want to minimize your contact with the ground.
- If on a mountain sit crosswise to the slope, and not in line with the slope.
- If next to walls, stand 6 feet away if possible, or as far away as you can get.
- If in a group of people, split up so you don't all get hit by one stroke. Get at least 15 feet apart from each other.
- It is OK to sit at the back of deep caves on a slope (don't touch the wall), but do not stand or sit in shallow caves as the lightning may flow through you.

Leiningen Versus the Ants

by Carl Stephenson

"Unless they alter their course and there's no reason why they should, they'll reach your plantation in two days at the latest."

Leiningen sucked placidly at a cigar about the size of a corn cob and for a few seconds gazed without answering at the agitated District Commissioner. Then he took the cigar from his lips, and leaned slightly forward. With his bristling grey hair, bulky nose, and lucid eyes, he had the look of an aging and shabby eagle.

"Decent of you," he murmured, "paddling all this way just to give me the tip. But you're pulling my leg of course when you say I must do a bunk. Why, even a herd of saurians couldn't drive me from this plantation of mine."

The Brazilian official threw up lean and lanky arms and clawed the air with wildly distended fingers. "Leiningen!" he shouted. "You're insane! They're not creatures you can fight—they're an elemental—an 'act of God!' Ten miles long, two miles wide—ants, nothing but ants! And every single one of them a fiend from hell; before you can spit three times they'll eat a full-grown buffalo to the bones. I tell you if you don't clear out at once there'll be nothing left of you but a skeleton picked as clean as your own plantation."

Leiningen grinned. "Act of God, my eye! Anyway, I'm not an old woman; I'm not going to run for it just because an elemental's on the way. And don't think I'm the kind of fathead who tries to fend off lightning with his fists, either. I use my intelligence, old man. With me, the brain isn't a second blind-gut; I know what it's there for. When I began this model farm and plantation three years ago, I took into account all that could conceivably happen to it. And now I'm ready for anything and everything—including your ants."

The Brazilian rose heavily to his feet. "I've done my best," he gasped. "Your obstinacy endangers not only yourself, but the lives of your four hundred workers. You don't know these ants!"

Leiningen accompanied him down to the river, where the Government launch was moored. The vessel cast off. As it moved downstream, the exclamation mark neared the rail and began waving its arms frantically. Long after the launch had disappeared round the bend, Leiningen thought he could still hear that dimming, imploring voice, "You don't know them, I tell you! *You don't know them!*"

But the reported enemy was by no means unfamiliar to the planter. Before he started to work on his settlement, he had lived long enough in the country to see for himself the fearful devastations sometimes wrought by these ravenous insects in their campaigns for food. But since then he had planned measures of defence accordingly, and these, he was convinced, were in every way adequate to withstand the approaching peril.

Moreover, during his three years as a planter, Leiningen had met and defeated drought, flood, plague and all other "acts of God" which had come against him—unlike his fellow-settlers in the district, who had made little or no resistance. This unbroken success he attributed solely to the observance of his lifelong motto: *The human brain needs only to become fully aware of its powers to conquer even the elements*. Dullards reeled senselessly and aimlessly into the abyss; cranks, however brilliant, lost their heads when circumstances suddenly altered or accelerated and ran into stone walls, sluggards drifted with the current until they were caught in whirlpools and dragged under. But such disasters, Leiningen contented, merely strengthened his argument that intelligence, directed aright, invariably makes man the master of his fate.

Yes, Leiningen had always known how to grapple with life. Even here, in this Brazilian wilderness, his brain had triumphed over every difficulty and danger it had so far encountered. First he had vanquished primal forces by cunning and organization, then he had enlisted the resources of modern science to increase miraculously the yield of his plantation. And now he was sure he would prove more than a match for the "irresistible" ants.

That same evening, however, Leiningen assembled his workers. He had no intention of waiting till the news reached their ears from other sources. Most of them had been born in the district; the cry "The ants are coming!" was to them an imperative signal for instant, panic-stricken flight, a spring for life itself. But so great was the Indians' trust in Leiningen, in Leiningen's word, and in Leiningen's wisdom, that they received his curt tidings, and his orders for the imminent struggle, with the calmness with which they were given. They waited, unafraid, alert, as if for the beginning of a new game or hunt which he had just described to them, the ants were indeed mighty, but not so mighty as the boss. Let them come!

They came at noon the second day. Their approach was announced by the wild unrest of the horses, scarcely controllable now either in stall or under rider, scenting from afar a vapor instinct with horror.

It was announced by a stampede of animals, timid and savage, hurtling past each other; jaguars and pumas flashing by nimble stags of the pampas, bulky tapirs, no longer hunters, themselves hunted, outpacing fleet kinkajous, maddened herds of cattle, heads lowered, nostrils snorting, rushing through tribes of loping monkeys, chattering in a dementia of terror; then followed the creeping and springing denizens of bush and steppe, big and little rodents, snakes and lizards.

Pell-mell the rabble swarmed down the hill to the plantation, scattered right and left before the barrier of the water-filled ditch, then sped onwards to the river, where, again hindered, they fled along its bank out of sight.

This water-filled ditch was one of the defence measures which Leiningen had long since prepared against the advent of the ants. It encompassed three sides of the plantation like a huge horseshoe. Twelve feet across, but not very deep, when dry it could hardly be described as an obstacle to either man or beast. But the ends of the "horseshoe" ran into the river which formed the northern boundary, and fourth side, of the plantation. And at the end nearer the house and outbuildings in the middle of the plantation, Leiningen had constructed a dam by means of which water from the river could be diverted into the ditch.

So now, by opening the dam, he was able to fling an imposing girdle of water, a huge quadrilateral with the river as its base, completely around the plantation, like the moat encircling a medieval city. Unless the ants were clever enough to build rafts, they had no hope of reaching the plantation, Leiningen concluded.

The twelve-foot water ditch seemed to afford in itself all the security needed. But while awaiting the arrival of the ants, Leiningen made a further improvement. The western section of the ditch ran along the edge of a tamarind wood, and the branches of some great trees reached over the water. Leiningen now had them lopped so that ants could not descend from them within the "moat."

The women and children, then the herds of cattle, were escorted by peons on rafts over the river, to remain on the other side in absolute safety until the plunderers had departed. Leiningen gave this instruction, not because he believed the non-combatants were in any danger, but in order to avoid hampering the efficiency of the defenders. "Critical situations first become crises," he explained to his men, "when oxen or women get excited."

Finally, he made a careful inspection of the "inner moat"—a smaller ditch lined with concrete, which extended around the hill on which stood the ranch house, barns, stables and other buildings. Into this concrete ditch emptied the inflow pipes from three great petrol tanks. If by some miracle the ants managed to cross the water and reach the plantation, this "rampart of petrol" would be an absolutely impassable protection for the besieged and their dwellings and stock. Such, at least, was Leiningen's opinion.

He stationed his men at irregular distances along the water ditch, the first line of defence. Then he lay down in his hammock and puffed drowsily away at his pipe until a peon came with the report that the ants had been observed far away in the South.

Leiningen mounted his horse, which at the feel of its master seemed to forget its uneasiness, and rode leisurely in the direction of the threatening offensive. The southern stretch of ditch—the upper side of the quadrilateral— was nearly three miles long; from its center one could survey the entire countryside. This was destined to be the scene of the outbreak of war between Leiningen's brain and twenty square miles of life-destroying ants.

It was a sight one could never forget. Over the range of hills, as far as eye could see, crept a darkening hem, ever longer and broader, until the shadow spread across the slope from east to west, then downwards, downwards, uncannily swift, and all the green herbage of that wide vista was being mown as by a giant sickle, leaving only the vast moving shadow, extending, deepening, and moving rapidly nearer.

When Leiningen's men, behind their barrier of water, perceived the approach of the long-expected foe, they gave vent to their suspense in screams and imprecations. But as the distance began to lessen between the "sons of hell" and the water ditch, they relapsed into silence. Before the advance of that awe-inspiring throng, their belief in the powers of the boss began to steadily dwindle.

Even Leiningen himself, who had ridden up just in time to restore their loss of heart by a display of unshakable calm, even he could not free himself from a qualm of malaise. Yonder were thousands of millions of voracious jaws bearing down upon him and only a suddenly insignificant, narrow ditch lay between him and his men and being gnawed to the bones "before you can spit three times."

Hadn't his brain for once taken on more than it could manage? If the blighters decided to rush the ditch, fill it to the brim with their corpses, there'd still be more than enough to destroy every trace of that cranium of his. The planter's chin jutted; they hadn't got him yet, and he'd see to it they never would. While he could think at all, he'd flout both death and the devil.

The hostile army was approaching in perfect formation; no human battalions, however well-drilled, could ever hope to rival the precision of that advance. Along a front that moved forward as uniformly as a straight line, the ants drew nearer and nearer to the water-ditch. Then, when they learned through their scouts the nature of the obstacle, the two outlying wings of the army detached themselves from the main body and marched down the western and eastern sides of the ditch.

This surrounding maneuver took rather more than an hour to accomplish; no doubt the ants expected that at some point they would find a crossing.

During this outflanking movement by the wings, the army on the center and southern front remained still. The besieged were therefore able to contemplate at their leisure the thumb-long, reddish black, long-legged insects; some of the Indians believed they could see, too, intent on them, the brilliant, cold eyes, and the razor-edged mandibles, of this host of infinity.

It is not easy for the average person to imagine that an animal, not to mention an insect, can *think*. But now both the European brain of Leiningen and the primitive brains of the Indians began to stir with the unpleasant foreboding that inside every single one of that deluge of insects dwelt a thought. And that thought was: Ditch or no ditch, we'll get to your flesh!

Not until four o'clock did the wings reach the "horseshoe" ends of the ditch, only to find these ran into the great river. Through some kind of secret telegraphy, the report must then have flashed very swiftly indeed along the entire enemy line. And Leiningen, riding—no longer casually—along his side of the ditch, noticed by energetic and widespread movements of troops that for some unknown reason the news of the check had its greatest effect on the southern front, where the main army was massed. Perhaps the failure to find a way over the ditch was persuading the ants to withdraw from the plantation in search of spoils more easily attainable.

An immense flood of ants, about a hundred yards in width, was pouring in a glimmering-black cataract down the far slope of the ditch. Many thousands were already drowning in the sluggish creeping flow, but they were followed by troop after troop, who clambered over their sinking comrades, and then themselves served as dying bridges to the reserves hurrying on in their rear.

Shoals of ants were being carried away by the current into the middle of the ditch, where gradually they broke asunder and then, exhausted by their struggles, vanished below the surface. Nevertheless, the wavering, floundering hundred-yard front was remorselessly if slowly advancing towards the besieged on the other bank. Leiningen had been wrong when he supposed the enemy would first have to fill the ditch with their bodies before they could cross; instead, they merely needed to act as stepping-stones, as they swam and sank, to the hordes ever pressing onwards from behind.

Near Leiningen a few mounted herdsmen awaited his orders. He sent one to the weir—the river must be damned more strongly to increase the speed and power of the water coursing through the ditch.

A second peon was dispatched to the outhouses to bring spades and petrol sprinklers. A third rode away to summon to the zone of the offensive all the men, except the observation posts, on the near-by section of the ditch, which were not yet actively threatened.

The ants were getting across far more quickly than Leiningen would have deemed possible. Impelled by the mighty cascade behind them, they struggled nearer and nearer to the inner bank. The momentum of the attack was so great that neither the tardy flow of the stream nor its downward pull could exert its proper force; and into the gap left by every submerging insect, hastened forward a dozen more.

When reinforcements reached Leiningen, the invaders were halfway over. The planter had to admit to himself that it was only by a stroke of luck for him that the ants were attempting the crossing on a relatively short front: had they assaulted simultaneously along the entire length of the ditch, the outlook for the defenders would have been black indeed.

Even as it was, it could hardly be described as rosy, though the planter seemed quite unaware that death in a gruesome form was drawing closer and closer. As the war between his brain and the "act of God" reached its climax, the very shadow of annihilation began to pale to Leiningen, who now felt like a champion in a new Olympic game, a gigantic and thrilling contest, from which he was determined to emerge victor. Such, indeed, was his aura of confidence that the Indians forgot their stupefied fear of the peril only a yard or two away; under the planter's supervision, they began fervidly digging up to the edge of the bank and throwing clods of earth and spadefuls of sand into the midst of the hostile fleet.

The petrol sprinklers, hitherto used to destroy pests and blights on the plantation, were also brought into action. Streams of evil-reeking oil now soared and fell over an enemy already in disorder through the bombardment of earth and sand.

The ants responded to these vigorous and successful measures of defence by further developments of their offensive. Entire clumps of huddling insects began to roll down the opposite bank into the water. At the same time, Leiningen noticed that the ants were now attacking along an ever-widening front. As the numbers both of his men and his petrol sprinklers were severely limited, this rapid extension of the line of battle was becoming an overwhelming danger.

To add to his difficulties, the very clods of earth they flung into that black floating carpet often whirled fragments towards the defenders' side, and here and there dark ribbons were already mounting the inner bank. True, wherever a man saw these they could still be driven back into the water by spadefuls of earth or jets of petrol. But the file of defenders was too sparse and scattered to hold off at all points these landing parties, and though the peons toiled like madmen, their plight became momently more perilous.

One man struck with his spade at an enemy clump, did not draw it back quickly enough from the water; in a trice the wooden haft swarmed with upward scurrying insects. With a curse, he dropped the spade into the ditch; too late, they were already on his body. They lost no time; wherever they encountered bare flesh they bit deeply; a few, bigger than the rest, carried in their hindquarters a sting which injected a burning and paralyzing venom. Screaming, frantic with pain, the peon danced and twirled like a dervish.

Realizing that another such casualty, yes, perhaps this alone, might plunge his men into confusion and destroy their morale, Leiningen roared in a bellow louder than the yells of the victim: "Into the petrol, idiot! Douse your paws in the petrol!" The dervish ceased his pirouette as if transfixed, then tore off his shirt and plunged his arm and the ants hanging to it up to the shoulder in one of the large open pits of petrol. But even then the fierce mandibles did not slacken; another peon had to help him squash and detach each separate insect.

Distracted by the episode, some defenders had turned away from the ditch. And now cries of fury, a thudding of spades, and a wild trampling to and fro, showed that the ants had made full use of the interval, though luckily only a few had managed to get across. The men set to work again desperately with the barrage of earth and sand. Meanwhile an old Indian, who acted as medicine-man to the plantation workers, gave the bitten peon a drink he had prepared some hours before, which, he claimed, possessed the virtue of dissolving and weakening ants' venom.

Leiningen surveyed his position. A dispassionate observer would have estimated the odds against him at a thousand to one. But then such an onlooker would have reckoned only by what he saw—the advance of myriad battalions of ants against the futile efforts of a few defenders—and not by the unseen activity that can go on in a man's brain.

For Leiningen had not erred when he decided he would fight elemental with elemental. The water in the ditch was beginning to rise; the stronger damming of the river was making itself apparent.

Visibly the swiftness and power of the masses of water increased, swirling into quicker and quicker movement its living black surface, dispersing its pattern, carrying away more and more of it on the hastening current.

Victory had been snatched from the very jaws of defeat. With a hysterical shout of joy, the peons feverishly intensified their bombardment of earth clods and sand.

And now the wide cataract down the opposite bank was thinning and ceasing, as if the ants were becoming aware that they could not attain their aim. They were scurrying back up the slope to safety

All the troops so far hurled into the ditch had been sacrificed in vain. Drowned and floundering insects eddied in thousands along the flow, while Indians running on the bank destroyed every swimmer that reached the side.

Not until the ditch curved towards the east did the scattered ranks assemble again in a coherent mass. And now, exhausted and half-numbed, they were in no condition to ascend the bank. Fusillades of clods drove them round the bend towards the mouth of the ditch and then into the river, wherein they vanished without leaving a trace.

The news ran swiftly along the entire chain of outposts, and soon a long scattered line of laughing men could be seen hastening along the ditch towards the scene of victory.

For once they seemed to have lost all their native reserve, for it was in wild abandon now they celebrated the triumph—as if there were no longer thousands of millions of merciless, cold and hungry eyes watching them from the opposite bank, watching and waiting.

The sun sank behind the rim of the tamarind wood and twilight deepened into night. It was not only hoped but expected that the ants would remain quiet until dawn. But to defeat any forlorn attempt at a crossing, the flow of water through the ditch was powerfully increased by opening the dam still further.

In spite of this impregnable barrier, Leiningen was not yet altogether convinced that the ants would not venture another surprise attack. He ordered his men to camp along the bank overnight. He also detailed parties of them to patrol the ditch in two of his motor cars and ceaselessly to illuminate the surface of the water with headlights and electric torches.

After having taken all the precautions he deemed necessary, the farmer ate his supper with considerable appetite and went to bed. His slumbers were in no wise disturbed by the memory of the waiting, live, twenty square miles.

Dawn found a thoroughly refreshed and active Leiningen riding along the edge of the ditch. The planter saw before him a motionless and unaltering throng of besiegers. He studied the wide belt of water between them and the plantation, and for a moment almost regretted that the fight had ended so soon and so simply. In the comforting, matter-of-fact light of morning, it seemed to him now that the ants hadn't the ghost of a chance to cross the ditch. Even if they plunged headlong into it on all three fronts at once, the force of the now powerful current would inevitably sweep them away. He had got quite a thrill out of the fight—a pity it was already over.

He rode along the eastern and southern sections of the ditch and found everything in order. He reached the western section, opposite the tamarind wood, and here, contrary to the other battle fronts, he found the enemy very busy indeed. The trunks and branches of the trees and the creepers of the lianas, on the far bank of the ditch, fairly swarmed with industrious insects. But instead of eating the leaves there and then, they were merely gnawing through the stalks, so that a thick green shower fell steadily to the ground.

No doubt they were victualing columns sent out to obtain provender for the rest of the army. The discovery did not surprise Leiningen. He did not need to be told that ants are intelligent, that certain species even use others as milch cows, watchdogs and slaves. He was well aware of their power of adaptation, their sense of discipline, their marvelous talent for organization.

His belief that a foray to supply the army was in progress was strengthened when he saw the leaves that fell to the ground being dragged to the troops waiting outside the wood. Then all at once he realized the aim that rain of green was intended to serve.

Each single leaf, pulled or pushed by dozens of toiling insects, was borne straight to the edge of the ditch. Even as Macbeth watched the approach of Birnam Wood in the hands of his enemies, Leiningen saw the tamarind wood move nearer and nearer in the mandibles of the ants. Unlike the fey Scot, however, he did not lose his nerve; no witches had prophesied his doom, and if they had he would have slept just as soundly. All the same, he was forced to admit to himself that the situation was now far more ominous than that of the day before.

He had thought it impossible for the ants to build rafts for themselves—well, here they were, coming in thousands, more than enough to bridge the ditch. Leaves after leaves rustled down the slope into the water, where the current drew them away from the bank and carried them into mid-stream. And every single leaf carried several ants. This time the farmer did not trust to the alacrity of his messengers. He galloped away, leaning from his saddle and yelling orders as he rushed past outpost after outpost: "Bring petrol pumps to the southwest front! Issue spades to every man along the line facing the wood!" And arrived at the eastern and southern sections, he dispatched every man except the observation posts to the menaced west.

Then, as he rode past the stretch where the ants had failed to cross the day before, he witnessed a brief but impressive scene. Down the slope of the distant hill there came towards him a singular being, writhing rather than running, an animal-like blackened statue with a shapeless head and four quivering feet that knuckled under almost ceaselessly. When the creature reached the far bank of the ditch and collapsed opposite Leiningen, he recognized it as a pampas stag, covered over and over with ants.

It had strayed near the zone of the army. As usual, they had attacked its eyes first. Blinded, it had reeled in the madness of hideous torment straight into the ranks of its persecutors, and now the beast swayed to and fro in its death agony.

With a shot from his rifle Leiningen put it out of its misery. Then he pulled out his watch. He hadn't a second to lose, but for life itself he could not have denied his curiosity the satisfaction of knowing how long the ants would take—for personal reasons, so to speak. After six minutes the white polished bones alone remained. That's how he himself would look before you can— Leiningen spat once, and put spurs to his horse.

The sporting zest with which the excitement of the novel contest had inspired him the day before had now vanished; in its place was a cold and violent purpose. He would send these vermin back to the hell where they belonged, somehow, anyhow. Yes, but how was indeed the question; as things stood at present it looked as if the devils would raze him and his men from the earth instead. He had underestimated the might of the enemy; he really would have to bestir himself if he hoped to outwit them.

The biggest danger now, he decided, was the point where the western section of the ditch curved southwards. And arrived there, he found his worst expectations justified. The very power of the current had huddled the leaves and their crews of ants so close together at the bend that the bridge was almost ready.

True, streams of petrol and clumps of earth still prevented a landing. But the number of floating leaves was increasing ever more swiftly. It could not be long now before a stretch of water a mile in length was decked by a green pontoon over which the ants could rush in millions.

Leiningen galloped to the weir. The damming of the river was controlled by a wheel on its bank. The planter ordered the man at the wheel first to lower the water in the ditch almost to vanishing point, next to wait a moment, then suddenly to let the river in again. This maneuver of lowering and raising the surface, of decreasing then increasing the flow of water through the ditch was to be repeated over and over again until further notice.

This tactic was at first successful. The water in the ditch sank, and with it the film of leaves. The green fleet nearly reached the bed and the troops on the far banks swarmed down the slope to it. Then a violent flow of water at the original depth raced through the ditch, overwhelming leaves and ants, and sweeping them along.

This intermittent rapid flushing prevented just in time the almost completed fording of the ditch. But it also flung here and there squads of the enemy vanguard simultaneously up the inner bank. These seemed to know their duty only too well, and lost no time accomplishing it. The air rang with the curses of bitten Indians. They had removed their shirts and pants to detect the quicker the upwards-hastening insects; when they saw one, they crushed it; and fortunately the onslaught as yet was only by skirmishers.

Again and again, the water sank and rose, carrying leaves and drowned ants away with it. It lowered once more nearly to its bed; but this time the exhausted defenders waited in vain for the flush of destruction. Leiningen sensed disaster; something must have gone wrong with the machinery of the dam. Then a sweating peon tore up to him—

"They're over!"

While the besieged were concentrating upon the defence of the stretch opposite the wood, the seemingly unaffected line beyond the wood had become the theatre of decisive action. Here the defenders' front was sparse and scattered; everyone who could be spared had hurried away to the south.

Just as the man at the weir had lowered the water almost to the bed of the ditch, the ants on a wide front began another attempt at a direct crossing like that of the preceding day. Into the emptied bed poured an irresistible throng. Rushing across the ditch, they attained the inner bank before the slow-witted Indians fully grasped the situation. Their frantic screams dumbfounded the man at the weir. Before he could direct the river anew into the safeguarding bed he saw himself surrounded by raging ants. He ran like the others, ran for his life.

When Leiningen heard this, he knew the plantation was doomed. He wasted no time bemoaning the inevitable. For as long as there was the slightest chance of success, he had stood his ground, and now any further resistance was both useless and dangerous. He fired three revolver shots into the air—the prearranged signal for his men to retreat instantly within the "inner moat." Then he rode towards the ranch house.

This was two miles from the point of invasion. There was therefore time enough to prepare the second line of defence against the advent of the ants. Of the three great petrol cisterns near the house, one had already been half emptied by the constant withdrawals needed for the pumps during the fight at the water ditch. The remaining petrol in it was now drawn off through underground pipes into the concrete trench which encircled the ranchhouse and its outbuildings.

And there, drifting in twos and threes, Leiningen's men reached him. Most of them were obviously trying to preserve an air of calm and indifference, belied, however, by their restless glances and knitted brows. One could see their belief in a favorable outcome of the struggle was already considerably shaken.

The planter called his peons around him.

"Well, lads," he began, "we've lost the first round. But we'll smash the beggars yet, don't you worry. Anyone who thinks otherwise can draw his pay here and now and push off. There are rafts enough and to spare on the river and plenty of time still to reach 'em."

Not a man stirred.

Leiningen acknowledged his silent vote of confidence with a laugh that was half a grunt. "That's the stuff, lads. Too bad if you'd missed the rest of the show, eh? Well, the fun won't start till morning. Once the blighters turn tail, there'll be plenty of work for everyone and higher wages all round. And now run along and get something to eat; you've earned it all right."

In the excitement of the fight the greater part of the day had passed without the men once pausing to snatch a bite. Now that the ants were for the time being out of sight, and the "wall of petrol" gave a stronger feeling of security, hungry stomachs began to assert their claims.

The bridges over the concrete ditch were removed. Here and there solitary ants had reached the ditch; they gazed at the petrol meditatively, then scurried back again. Apparently they had little interest at the moment for what lay beyond the evil-reeking barrier; the abundant spoils of the plantation were the main attraction. Soon the trees, shrubs and beds for miles around were hulled with ants zealously gobbling the yield of long weary months of strenuous toil.

As twilight began to fall, a cordon of ants marched around the petrol trench, but as yet made no move towards its brink. Leiningen posted sentries with headlights and electric torches, then withdrew to his office, and began to reckon up his losses. He estimated these as large, but, in comparison with his bank balance, by no means unbearable. He worked out in some detail a scheme of intensive cultivation which would enable him, before very long, to more than compensate himself for the damage now being wrought to his crops. It was with a contented mind that he finally betook himself to bed where he slept deeply until dawn, undisturbed by any thought that next day little more might be left of him than a glistening skeleton.

He rose with the sun and went out on the flat roof of his house. And a scene like one from Dante lay around him; for miles in every direction there was nothing but a black, glittering multitude, a multitude of rested, sated, but none the less voracious ants: yes, look as far as one might, one could see nothing but that rustling black throng, except in the north, where the great river drew a boundary they could not hope to pass. But even the high stone break-water, along the bank of the river, which Leiningen had built as a defence against inundations, was, like the paths, the shorn trees and shrubs, the ground itself, black with ants.

So their greed was not glutted in razing that vast plantation? Not by a long chalk; they were all the more eager now on a rich and certain booty— four hundred men, numerous horses, and bursting granaries.

At first it seemed that the petrol trench would serve its purpose. The besiegers sensed the peril of swimming it, and made no move to plunge blindly over its brink. Instead they devised a better maneuver; they began to collect shreds of bark, twigs and dried leaves and dropped these into the petrol. Everything green, which could have been similarly used, had long since been eaten.

After a time, though, a long procession could be seen bringing from the west the tamarind leaves used as rafts the day before.

Since the petrol, unlike the water in the outer ditch, was perfectly still, the refuse stayed where it was thrown. It was several hours before the ants succeeded in covering an appreciable part of the surface. At length, however, they were ready to proceed to a direct attack.

Their storm troops swarmed down the concrete side, scrambled over the supporting surface of twigs and leaves, and impelled these over the few remaining streaks of open petrol until they reached the other side. Then they began to climb up this to make straight for the helpless garrison.

During the entire offensive, the planter sat peacefully, watching them with interest, but not stirring a muscle. Moreover, he had ordered his men not to disturb in any way whatever the advancing horde. So they squatted listlessly along the bank of the ditch and waited for a sign from the boss.

The petrol was now covered with ants. A few had climbed the inner concrete wall and were scurrying towards the defenders.

"Everyone back from the ditch!" roared Leiningen. The men rushed away, without the slightest idea of his plan. He stooped forward and cautiously dropped into the ditch a stone which split the floating carpet and its living freight, to reveal a gleaming patch of petrol. A match spurted, sank down to the oily surface—Leiningen sprang back; in a flash a towering rampart of fire encompassed the garrison.

This spectacular and instant repulse threw the Indians into ecstasy. They applauded, yelled and stamped, like children at a pantomime. Had it not been for the awe in which they held the boss, they would infallibly have carried him shoulder high.

It was some time before the petrol burned down to the bed of the ditch, and the wall of smoke and flame began to lower, The ants had retreated in a wide circle from the devastation, and innumerable charred fragments along the outer bank showed that the flames had spread from the holocaust in the ditch well into the ranks beyond, where they had wrought havoc far and wide.

Yet the perseverance of the ants was by no means broken; indeed, each setback seemed only to whet it. The concrete cooled, the flicker of the dying flames wavered and vanished, petrol from the second tank poured into the trench and the ants marched forward anew to the attack.

The foregoing scene repeated itself in every detail, except that on this occasion less time was needed to bridge the ditch, for the petrol was now already filmed by a layer of ash. Once again they withdrew; once again petrol flowed into the ditch. Would the creatures never learn that their self-sacrifice was utterly senseless? It really was senseless, wasn't it? Yes, of course it was senseless—provided the defenders had an *unlimited* supply of petrol.

When Leiningen reached this stage of reasoning, he felt for the first time since the arrival of the ants that his confidence was deserting him. His skin began to creep; he loosened his collar. Once the devils were over the trench there wasn't a chance in hell for him and his men. God, what a prospect, to be eaten alive like that!

For the third time the flames immolated the attacking troops, and burned down to extinction. Yet the ants were coming on again as if nothing had happened. And meanwhile Leiningen had made a discovery that chilled him to the bone—petrol was no longer flowing into the ditch. Something must be blocking the outflow pipe of the third and last cistern—a snake or a dead rat? Whatever it was, the ants could be held off no longer, unless petrol could by some method be led from the cistern into the ditch.

Then Leiningen remembered that in an outhouse near-by were two old disused fire engines. Spry as never before in their lives, the peons dragged them out of the shed, connected their pumps to the cistern, uncoiled and laid the hose. They were just in time to aim a stream of petrol at a column of ants that had already crossed and drive them back down the incline into the ditch. Once more an oily girdle surrounded the garrison, once more it was possible to hold the position—for the moment.

It was obvious, however, that this last resource meant only the postponement of defeat and death. A few of the peons fell on their knees and began to pray; others, shrieking insanely, fired their revolvers at the black, advancing masses, as if they felt their despair was pitiful enough to sway fate itself to mercy.

At length, two of the men's nerves broke: Leiningen saw a naked Indian leap over the north side of the petrol trench, quickly followed by a second. They sprinted with incredible speed towards the river. But their fleetness did not save them; long before they could attain the rafts, the enemy covered their bodies from head to foot.

In the agony of their torment, both sprang blindly into the wide river, where enemies no less sinister awaited them. Wild screams of mortal anguish informed the breathless onlookers that crocodiles and sword-toothed piranhas were no less ravenous than ants, and even nimbler in reaching their prey.

In spite of this bloody warning, more and more men showed they were making up their minds to run the blockade. Anything, even a fight mid-stream against alligators, seemed better than powerlessly waiting for death to come and slowly consume their living bodies.

Leiningen flogged his brain till it reeled. Was there nothing on earth could sweep this devils' spawn back into the hell from which it came?

Then out of the inferno of his bewilderment rose a terrifying inspiration. Yes, one hope remained, and one alone. It might be possible to dam the great river completely, so that its waters would fill not only the water ditch but overflow into the entire gigantic "saucer" of land in which lay the plantation.

The far bank of the river was too high for the waters to escape that way. The stone breakwater ran between the river and the plantation; its only gaps occurred where the "horseshoe" ends of the water-ditch passed into the river. So its waters would not only be forced to inundate into the plantation, they would also be held there by the breakwater until they rose to its own high level. In half an hour, perhaps even earlier, the plantation and its hostile army of occupation would be flooded.

The ranch house and outbuildings stood upon rising ground. Their foundations were higher than the breakwater, so the flood would not reach them. And any remaining ants trying to ascend the slope could be repulsed by petrol.

It was possible—yes, if one could only get to the dam! A distance of nearly two miles lay between the ranch house and the weir—two miles of ants. Those two peons had managed only a fifth of that distance at the cost of their lives. Was there an Indian daring enough after that to run the gauntlet five times as far? Hardly likely; and if there were, his prospect of getting back was almost nil.

No, there was only one thing for it, he'd have to make the attempt himself; he might just as well be running as sitting still, anyway, when the ants finally got him. Besides, there *was* a bit of a chance. Perhaps the ants weren't so almighty, after all; perhaps he had allowed the mass suggestion of that evil black throng to hypnotize him, just as a snake fascinates and overpowers.

The ants were building their bridges. Leiningen got up on a chair. "Hey, lads, listen to me!" he cried. Slowly and listlessly, from all sides of the trench, the men began to shuffle towards him, the apathy of death already stamped on their faces.

"Listen, lads!" he shouted. "You're frightened of those beggars, but you're a damn sight more frightened of me, and I'm proud of you. There's still a chance to save our lives—by flooding the plantation from the river. Now one of you might manage to get as far as the weir—but he'd never come back. Well, I'm not going to let you try it; if I did I'd be worse than one of those ants. No, I called the tune, and now I'm going to pay the piper.

"The moment I'm over the ditch, set fire to the petrol. That'll allow time for the flood to do the trick. Then all you have to do is to wait here all snug and quiet till I'm back. Yes, I'm coming back, trust me"—he grinned— "when I've finished my slimming-cure."

He pulled on high leather boots, drew heavy gauntlets over his hands, and stuffed the spaces between breeches and boots, gauntlets and arms, shirt and neck, with rags soaked in petrol. With close-fitting mosquito goggles he shielded his eyes, knowing too well the ants' dodge of first robbing their victim of sight. Finally, he plugged his nostrils and ears with cotton-wool, and let the peons drench his clothes with petrol.

He was about to set off, when the old Indian medicine man came up to him; he had a wondrous salve, he said, prepared from a species of chafer whose odor was intolerable to ants. Yes, this odor protected these chafers from the attacks of even the most murderous ants. The Indian smeared the boss' boots, his gauntlets, and his face over and over with the extract.

Leiningen then remembered the paralyzing effect of ants' venom, and the Indian gave him a gourd full of medicine he had administered to the bitten peon at the water ditch. The planter drank it down without noticing its bitter taste; his mind was already at the weir.

He started off towards the northwest corner of the trench. With a bound he was over—and among the ants.

The beleaguered garrison had no opportunity to watch Leiningen's race against death. The ants were climbing the inner bank again—the lurid ring of petrol blazed aloft. For the fourth time that day the reflection from the fire shone on the sweating faces of the imprisoned men, and on the reddish- black cuirasses of their oppressors. The red and blue, dark-edged flames leaped vividly now, celebrating what? The funeral pyre of the four hundred, or of the hosts of destruction?

Leiningen ran. He ran in long, equal strides, with only one thought, one sensation, in his being—he *must* get through. He dodged all trees and shrubs; except for the split seconds his soles touched the ground the ants should have no opportunity to alight on him. That they would get to him soon, despite the salve on his boots, the petrol in his clothes, he realized only too well, but he knew even more surely that he must, and that he would, get to the weir.

Apparently the salve was some use after all; not until he had reached halfway did he feel ants under his clothes, and a few on his face. Mechanically, in his stride, he struck at them, scarcely conscious of their bites. He saw he was drawing appreciably nearer the weir—the distance grew less and less—sank to five hundred—three—two—one hundred yards.

Then he was at the weir and gripping the ant-hulled wheel. Hardly had he seized it when a horde of infuriated ants flowed over his hands, arms and shoulders. He started the wheel—before it turned once on its axis the swarm covered his face. Leiningen strained like a madman, his lips pressed tight; if he opened them to draw breath...

He turned and turned; slowly the dam lowered until it reached the bed of the river. Already the water was overflowing the ditch. Another minute and the river was pouring through the near-by gap in the breakwater. The flooding of the plantation had begun.

Leiningen let go the wheel. Now, for the first time, he realized he was coated from head to foot with a layer of ants. In spite of the petrol, his clothes were full of them, several had got to his body or were clinging to his face. Now that he had completed his task, he felt the smart raging over his flesh from the bites of sawing and piercing insects.

Frantic with pain, he almost plunged into the river. To be ripped and slashed to shreds by piranhas? Already he was running the return journey, knocking ants from his gloves and jacket, brushing them from his bloodied face, squashing them to death under his clothes.

One of the creatures bit him just below the rim of his goggles; he managed to tear it away, but the agony of the bite and its etching acid drilled into the eye nerves; he saw now through circles of fire into a milky mist, then he ran for a time almost blinded, knowing that if he once tripped and fell... The old Indian's brew didn't seem much good; it weakened the poison a bit, but didn't get rid of it. His heart pounded as if it would burst; blood roared in his ears; a giant's fist battered his lungs.

Then he could see again, but the burning girdle of petrol appeared infinitely far away; he could not last half that distance. Swift-changing pictures flashed through his head, episodes in his life, while in another part of his brain a cool and impartial onlooker informed this ant-blurred, gasping, exhausted bundle named Leiningen that such a rushing panorama of scenes from one's past is seen only in the moment before death.

A stone in the path...too weak to avoid it...the planter stumbled and collapsed. He tried to rise...he must be pinned under a rock...it was impossible...the slightest movement was impossible.

Then all at once he saw, starkly clear and huge, and, right before his eyes, furred with ants, towering and swaying in its death agony, the pampas stag. In six minutes—gnawed to the bones. God, he *couldn't* die like that! And something outside him seemed to drag him to his feet. He tottered. He began to stagger forward again.

Through the blazing ring hurtled an apparition which, as soon as it reached the ground on the inner side, fell full length and did not move. Leiningen, at the moment he made that leap through the flames, lost consciousness for the first time in his life. As he lay there, with glazing eyes and lacerated face, he appeared a man returned from the grave. The peons rushed to him, stripped off his clothes, tore away the ants from a body that seemed almost one open wound; in some places the bones were showing. They carried him into the ranch house.

As the curtain of flame lowered, one could see in place of the illimitable host of ants an extensive vista of water. The thwarted river had swept over the plantation, carrying with it the entire army. The water had collected and mounted in the great "saucer," while the ants had in vain attempted to reach the hill on which stood the ranch house. The girdle of flames held them back.

And so imprisoned between water and fire, they had been delivered into the annihilation that was their god. And near the farther mouth of the water-ditch, where the stone mole had its second gap, the ocean swept the lost battalions into the river, to vanish forever.

The ring of fire dwindled as the water mounted to the petrol trench, and quenched the dimming flames. The inundation rose higher and higher: because its outflow was impeded by the timber and underbrush it had carried along with it, its surface required some time to reach the top of the high stone breakwater and discharge over it the rest of the shattered army.

It swelled over ant-stippled shrubs and bushes, until it washed against the foot of the knoll whereon the besieged had taken refuge. For a while an alluvial of ants tried again and again to attain this dry land, only to be repulsed by streams of petrol back into the merciless flood.

Leiningen lay on his bed, his body swathed from head to foot in bandages. With fomentations and salves, they had managed to stop the bleeding, and had dressed his many wounds. Now they thronged around him, one question in every face. Would he recover? "He won't die," said the old man who had bandaged him, "if he doesn't want to."

The planter opened his eyes. "Everything in order?" he asked.

"They're gone," said his nurse. "To hell." He held out to his master a gourd full of a powerful sleeping draught. Leiningen gulped it down.

"I told you I'd come back," he murmured, "even if I am a bit stream-lined." He grinned and shut his eyes. He slept.

TIPS FOR THE TRAIL

First Aid - Burns

1st Degree = Superficial; red skin; no blisters; only outermost layer of skin is burned; sunburn is an example.

2nd Degree = Deeper burn; redness; blisters; very painful.

3rd Degree = Very serious; all skin layers are burned; not painful because nerves are destroyed; dry; leathery; needs grafting.

1. Cool the burn by placing it in cool/cold water for up to 30 minutes. Do this as soon as possible.
2. Don't apply grease or butter - that's an old wife's tale.
3. Don't pull off any clothing that is stuck to the burn. You can cut off the edges of any cloth that is stuck.
4. Prevent infection by covering the burns with a sterile dressing as soon as possible.
5. Don't break any blisters--they will protect the burn.
6. Give the vicitim plenty of fluids.
7. 2nd degree burns of 10% or more of the body, or 3rd degree burns of 5% or more of body, are serious. Get medical help.

An Occurrence At Owl Creek Bridge
by Ambrose Bierce

A man stood upon a railroad bridge in northern Alabama, looking down into the swift water twenty feet below. The man's hands were behind his back, the wrists bound with a cord. A rope closely encircled his neck. It was attached to a stout cross-timber above his head and the slack fell to the level of his knees. Some loose boards laid upon the ties supporting the rails of the railway supplied a footing for him and his executioners—two private soldiers of the Federal army, directed by a sergeant who in civil life may have been a deputy sheriff. At a short remove upon the same temporary platform was an officer in the uniform of his rank, armed. He was a captain. A sentinel at each end of the bridge stood with his rifle in the position known as "support," that is to say, vertical in front of the left shoulder, the hammer resting on the forearm thrown straight across the chest—a formal and unnatural position, enforcing an erect carriage of the body. It did not appear to be the duty of these two men to know what was occurring at the center of the bridge; they merely blockaded the two ends of the foot planking that traversed it.

Beyond one of the sentinels nobody was in sight; the railroad ran straight away into a forest for a hundred yards, then, curving, was lost to view. Doubtless there was an outpost farther along. The other bank of the stream was open ground—a gentle slope topped with a stockade of vertical tree trunks, loopholed for rifles, with a single embrasure through which protruded the muzzle of a brass cannon commanding the bridge. Midway up the slope between the bridge and fort were the spectators—a single company of infantry in line, at "parade rest," the butts of their rifles on the ground, the barrels inclining slightly backward against the right shoulder, the hands crossed upon the stock.

A lieutenant stood at the right of the line, the point of his sword upon the ground, his left hand resting upon his right. Excepting the group of four at the center of the bridge, not a man moved. The company faced the bridge, staring stonily, motionless. The sentinels, facing the banks of the stream, might have been statues to adorn the bridge. The captain stood with folded arms, silent, observing the work of his subordinates, but making no sign.

Death is a dignitary who when he comes announced is to be received with formal manifestations of respect, even by those most familiar with him. In the code of military etiquette silence and fixity are forms of deference.

The man who was engaged in being hanged was apparently about thirty-five years of age. He was a civilian, if one might judge from his habit, which was that of a planter. His features were good—a straight nose, firm mouth, broad forehead, from which his long, dark hair was combed straight back, falling behind his ears to the collar of his well fitting frock coat. He wore a moustache and pointed beard, but no whiskers; his eyes were large and dark gray, and had a kindly expression which one would hardly have expected in one whose neck was in the hemp. Evidently this was no vulgar assassin. The liberal military code makes provision for hanging many kinds of persons, and gentlemen are not excluded.

The preparations being complete, the two private soldiers stepped aside and each drew away the plank upon which he had been standing. The sergeant turned to the captain, saluted and placed himself immediately behind that officer, who in turn moved apart one pace. These movements left the condemned man and the sergeant standing on the two ends of the same plank, which spanned three of the cross-ties of the bridge. The end upon which the civilian stood almost, but not quite, reached a fourth. This plank had been held in place by the weight of the captain; it was now held by that of the sergeant. At a signal from the former the latter would step aside, the plank would tilt and the condemned man go down between two ties. The arrangement commended itself to his judgement as simple and effective. His face had not been covered nor his eyes bandaged. He looked a moment at his "unsteadfast footing," then let his gaze wander to the swirling water of the stream racing madly beneath his feet.

A piece of dancing driftwood caught his attention and his eyes followed it down the current. How slowly it appeared to move! What a sluggish stream!

He closed his eyes in order to fix his last thoughts upon his wife and children. The water, touched to gold by the early sun, the brooding mists under the banks at some distance down the stream, the fort, the soldiers, the piece of drift—all had distracted him. And now he became conscious of a new disturbance. Striking through the thought of his dear ones was sound which he could neither ignore nor understand, a sharp, distinct, metallic percussion like the stroke of a blacksmith's hammer upon the anvil; it had the same ringing quality. He wondered what it was, and whether immeasurably distant or near by—it seemed both. Its recurrence was regular, but as slow as the tolling of a death knell. He awaited each new stroke with impatience and—he knew not why—apprehension. The intervals of silence grew progressively longer; the delays became maddening. With their greater infrequency the sounds increased in strength and sharpness. They hurt his ear like the trust of a knife; he feared he would shriek. What he heard was the ticking of his watch.

He unclosed his eyes and saw again the water below him. "If I could free my hands," he thought, "I might throw off the noose and spring into the stream. By diving I could evade the bullets and, swimming vigorously, reach the bank, take to the woods and get away home. My home, thank God, is as yet outside their lines; my wife and little ones are still beyond the invader's farthest advance."

As these thoughts, which have here to be set down in words, were flashed into the doomed man's brain rather than evolved from it the captain nodded to the sergeant. The sergeant stepped aside.

II

Peyton Fahrquhar was a well to do planter, of an old and highly respected Alabama family. Being a slave owner and like other slave owners a politician, he was naturally an original secessionist and ardently devoted to the Southern cause. Circumstances of an imperious nature, which it is unnecessary to relate here, had prevented him from taking service with that gallant army which had fought the disastrous campaigns ending with the fall of Corinth, and he chafed under the inglorious restraint, longing for the release of his energies, the larger life of the soldier, the opportunity for distinction. That opportunity, he felt, would come, as it comes to all in wartime. Meanwhile he did what he could. No service was too humble for him to perform in the aid of the South, no adventure to perilous for him to undertake if consistent with the character of a civilian who was at heart a soldier, and who in good faith and without too much qualification assented to at least a part of the frankly villainous dictum that all is fair in love and war.

One evening while Fahrquhar and his wife were sitting on a rustic bench near the entrance to his grounds, a gray-clad soldier rode up to the gate and asked for a drink of water.

Mrs. Fahrquhar was only too happy to serve him with her own white hands. While she was fetching the water her husband approached the dusty horseman and inquired eagerly for news from the front.

"The Yanks are repairing the railroads," said the man, "and are getting ready for another advance. They have reached the Owl Creek bridge, put it in order and built a stockade on the north bank. The commandant has issued an order, which is posted everywhere, declaring that any civilian caught interfering with the railroad, its bridges, tunnels, or trains will be summarily hanged. I saw the order."

"How far is it to the Owl Creek bridge?" Fahrquhar asked.

"About thirty miles."

"Is there no force on this side of the creek?"

"Only a picket post half a mile out, on the railroad, and a single sentinel at this end of the bridge."

"Suppose a man—a civilian and student of hanging—should elude the picket post and perhaps get the better of the sentinel," said Fahrquhar, smiling, "what could he accomplish?"

The soldier reflected. "I was there a month ago," he replied. "I observed that the flood of last winter had lodged a great quantity of driftwood against the wooden pier at this end of the bridge. It is now dry and would burn like tinder."

The lady had now brought the water, which the soldier drank. He thanked her ceremoniously, bowed to her husband and rode away. An hour later, after nightfall, he repassed the plantation, going northward in the direction from which he had come. He was a Federal scout.

III

As Peyton Fahrquhar fell straight downward through the bridge he lost consciousness and was as one already dead. From this state he was awakened—ages later, it seemed to him—by the pain of a sharp pressure upon his throat, followed by a sense of suffocation. Keen, poignant agonies seemed to shoot from his neck downward through every fiber of his body and limbs. These pains appeared to flash along well defined lines of ramification and to beat with an inconceivably rapid periodicity. They seemed like streams of pulsating fire heating him to an intolerable temperature. As to his head, he was conscious of nothing but a feeling of fullness—of congestion. These sensations were unaccompanied by thought. The intellectual part of his nature was already effaced; he had power only to feel, and feeling was torment. He was conscious of motion.

Encompassed in a luminous cloud, of which he was now merely the fiery heart, without material substance, he swung through unthinkable arcs of oscillation, like a vast pendulum. Then all at once, with terrible suddenness, the light about him shot upward with the noise of a loud splash; a frightful roaring was in his ears, and all was cold and dark. The power of thought was restored; he knew that the rope had broken and he had fallen into the stream. There was no additional strangulation; the noose about his neck was already suffocating him and kept the water from his lungs. To die of hanging at the bottom of a river!—the idea seemed to him ludicrous. He opened his eyes in the darkness and saw above him a gleam of light, but how distant, how inaccessible! He was still sinking, for the light became fainter and fainter until it was a mere glimmer. Then it began to grow and brighten, and he knew that he was rising toward the surface—knew it with reluctance, for he was now very comfortable. "To be hanged and drowned," he thought, "that is not so bad; but I do not wish to be shot. No; I will not be shot; that is not fair."

He was not conscious of an effort, but a sharp pain in his wrist apprised him that he was trying to free his hands. He gave the struggle his attention, as an idler might observe the feat of a juggler, without interest in the outcome. What splendid effort!—what magnificent, what superhuman strength! Ah, that was a fine endeavor! Bravo! The cord fell away; his arms parted and floated upward, the hands dimly seen on each side in the growing light. He watched them with a new interest as first one and then the other pounced upon the noose at his neck. They tore it away and thrust it fiercely aside, its undulations resembling those of a water snake. "Put it back, put it back!" He thought he shouted these words to his hands, for the undoing of the noose had been succeeded by the direst pang that he had yet experienced. His neck ached horribly; his brain was on fire, his heart, which had been fluttering faintly, gave a great leap, trying to force itself out at his mouth. His whole body was racked and wrenched with an insupportable anguish!

But his disobedient hands gave no heed to the command. They beat the water vigorously with quick, downward strokes, forcing him to the surface. He felt his head emerge; his eyes were blinded by the sunlight; his chest expanded convulsively, and with a supreme and crowning agony his lungs engulfed a great draught of air, which instantly he expelled in a shriek!

He was now in full possession of his physical senses. They were, indeed, preternaturally keen and alert. Something in the awful disturbance of his organic system had so exalted and refined them that they made record of things never before perceived. He felt the ripples upon his face and heard their separate sounds as they struck. He looked at the forest on the bank of the stream, saw the individual trees, the leaves and the veining of each leaf—he saw the very insects upon them: the locusts, the brilliant bodied flies, the gray spiders stretching their webs from twig to twig. He noted the prismatic colors in all the dewdrops upon a million blades of grass. The humming of the gnats that danced above the eddies of the stream, the beating of the dragon flies' wings, the strokes of the water spiders' legs, like oars which had lifted their boat—all these made audible music. A fish slid along beneath his eyes and he heard the rush of its body parting the water.

He had come to the surface facing down the stream; in a moment the visible world seemed to wheel slowly round, himself the pivotal point, and he saw the bridge, the fort, the soldiers upon the bridge, the captain, the sergeant, the two privates, his executioners. They were in silhouette against the blue sky. They shouted and gesticulated, pointing at him. The captain had drawn his pistol, but did not fire; the others were unarmed. Their movements were grotesque and horrible, their forms gigantic.

Suddenly he heard a sharp report and something struck the water smartly within a few inches of his head, spattering his face with spray. He heard a second report, and saw one of the sentinels with his rifle at his shoulder, a light cloud of blue smoke rising from the muzzle. The man in the water saw the eye of the man on the bridge gazing into his own through the sights of the rifle. He observed that it was a gray eye and remembered having read that gray eyes were keenest, and that all famous marksmen had them. Nevertheless, this one had missed.

A counter-swirl had caught Fahrquhar and turned him half round; he was again looking at the forest on the bank opposite the fort. The sound of a clear, high voice in a monotonous singsong now rang out behind him and came across the water with a distinctness that pierced and subdued all other sounds, even the beating of the ripples in his ears.

Although no soldier, he had frequented camps enough to know the dread significance of that deliberate, drawling, aspirated chant; the lieutenant on shore was taking a part in the morning's work. How coldly and pitilessly––with what an even, calm intonation, presaging, and enforcing tranquility in the men—with what accurately measured interval fell those cruel words:

"Company! . . . Attention! . . . Shoulder arms! . . . Ready! . . . Aim! . . . Fire!"

Fahrquhar dived—dived as deeply as he could. The water roared in his ears like the voice of Niagara, yet he heard the dull thunder of the volley and, rising again toward the surface, met shining bits of metal, singularly flattened, oscillating slowly downward. Some of them touched him on the face and hands, then fell away, continuing their descent.

One lodged between his collar and neck; it was uncomfortably warm and he snatched it out.

As he rose to the surface, gasping for breath, he saw that he had been a long time under water; he was perceptibly farther downstream—nearer to safety. The soldiers had almost finished reloading; the metal ramrods flashed all at once in the sunshine as they were drawn from the barrels, turned in the air, and thrust into their sockets. The two sentinels fired again, independently and ineffectually.

The hunted man saw all this over his shoulder; he was now swimming vigorously with the current. His brain was as energetic as his arms and legs; he thought with the rapidity of lightning:

"The officer," he reasoned, "will not make that martinet's error a second time. It is as easy to dodge a volley as a single shot. He has probably already given the command to fire at will. God help me, I cannot dodge them all!"

An appalling splash within two yards of him was followed by a loud, rushing sound, *diminuendo*, which seemed to travel back through the air to the fort and died in an explosion which stirred the very river to its deeps! A rising sheet of water curved over him, fell down upon him, blinded him, strangled him! The cannon had taken an hand in the game. As he shook his head free from the commotion of the smitten water he heard the deflected shot humming through the air ahead, and in an instant it was cracking and smashing the branches in the forest beyond.

"They will not do that again," he thought; "the next time they will use a charge of grape. I must keep my eye upon the gun; the smoke will apprise me—the report arrives too late; it lags behind the missile. That is a good gun."

Suddenly he felt himself whirled round and round—spinning like a top. The water, the banks, the forests, the now distant bridge, fort and men, all were commingled and blurred. Objects were represented by their colors only; circular horizontal streaks of color—that was all he saw.

He had been caught in a vortex and was being whirled on with a velocity of advance and gyration that made him giddy and sick. In few moments he was flung upon the gravel at the foot of the left bank of the stream—the southern bank—and behind a projecting point which concealed him from his enemies. The sudden arrest of his motion, the abrasion of one of his hands on the gravel, restored him, and he wept with delight. He dug his fingers into the sand, threw it over himself in handfuls and audibly blessed it. It looked like diamonds, rubies, emeralds; he could think of nothing beautiful which it did not resemble. The trees upon the bank were giant garden plants; he noted a definite order in their arrangement, inhaled the fragrance of their blooms. A strange roseate light shone through the spaces among their trunks and the wind made in their branches the music of Aeolian harps. He had not wish to perfect his escape—he was content to remain in that enchanting spot until retaken.

A whiz and a rattle of grapeshot among the branches high above his head roused him from his dream. The baffled cannoneer had fired him a random farewell. He sprang to his feet, rushed up the sloping bank, and plunged into the forest.

All that day he traveled, laying his course by the rounding sun. The forest seemed interminable; nowhere did he discover a break in it, not even a woodman's road. He had not known that he lived in so wild a region. There was something uncanny in the revelation.

By nightfall he was fatigued, footsore, famished. The thought of his wife and children urged him on. At last he found a road which led him in what he knew to be the right direction. It was as wide and straight as a city street, yet it seemed untraveled. No fields bordered it, no dwelling anywhere. Not so much as the barking of a dog suggested human habitation. The black bodies of the trees formed a straight wall on both sides, terminating on the horizon in a point, like a diagram in a lesson in perspective. Overhead, as he looked up through this rift in the wood, shone great golden stars looking unfamiliar and grouped in strange constellations. He was sure they were arranged in some order which had a secret and malign significance. The wood on either side was full of singular noises, among which—once, twice, and again—he distinctly heard whispers in an unknown tongue.

His neck was in pain and lifting his hand to it found it horribly swollen. He knew that it had a circle of black where the rope had bruised it. His eyes felt congested; he could no longer close them. His tongue was swollen with thirst; he relieved its fever by thrusting it forward from between his teeth into the cold air. How softly the turf had carpeted the untraveled avenue—he could no longer feel the roadway beneath his feet!

Doubtless, despite his suffering, he had fallen asleep while walking, for now he sees another scene—perhaps he has merely recovered from a delirium. He stands at the gate of his own home. All is as he left it, and all bright and beautiful in the morning sunshine. He must have traveled the entire night. As he pushes open the gate and passes up the wide white walk, he sees a flutter of female garments; his wife, looking fresh and cool and sweet, steps down from the veranda to meet him. At the bottom of the steps she stands waiting, with a smile of ineffable joy, an attitude of matchless grace and dignity. Ah, how beautiful she is! He springs forwards with extended arms. As he is about to clasp her he feels a stunning blow upon the back of the neck; a blinding white light blazes all about him with a sound like the shock of a cannon—then all is darkness and silence!

Peyton Fahrquhar was dead; his body, with a broken neck, swung gently from side to side beneath the timbers of the Owl Creek bridge.

TIPS FOR THE TRAIL

What to Do...When Crossing a Stream

1. If two streams meet, cross above the meeting place.
2. Wading is usually safer than jumping on slippery rocks or logs. Use a walking stick if you have one, or make one.
3. If the stream is fed by melting snow, cross in the morning.
4. Meandering streams are slower; cross where stream is widest.
5. Place sleeping bag/clothes in waterproof bag. Keep your pack on loosely so you can drop it if you get in trouble.
6. DO NOT tie a rope to anyone crossing the stream--they might be pulled under. If you have a rope across the stream, you can hold onto it when crossing but be downstream from rope.
7. Cross fast-moving streams at an angle upstream--cross slow-moving streams at a downstream angle. Keep your shoes on.
8. When crossing, drag your legs instead of lifting them.

TIPS FOR THE TRAIL

What to Do...When Caught by a Forest Fire

Be Prepared

- As soon as you detect a fire or smell smoke, prepare to leave.
- Travel downhill as much as possible as fires can move uphill several times faster. Avoid steep canyons and slopes.
- Don't wear synthetic material--put on wool or cotton.
- Discard your stove fuel and canisters.

If Caught

- Don't take chances--a fire can travel faster than you can run.
- Don't wet clothing--the water can turn to steam and scald you.
- Take shallow breaths through a dry (not wet) cloth.
- If you can, you can jump a low fire front into the relative safety of the burned area behind.
- If the fire catches you, lie face down on the ground. Cover yourself with dry dirt/sand or with a non-synthetic blanket.
- Stay calm!

TIPS FOR THE TRAIL

How to Pick a Good Campsite

Bad Sites

- Windy hilltops.
- Valley bottoms that might get cold and damp.
- Terraces that may be wet.
- Paths leading to water that animals may use.
- Trees that have dead branches that could fall in the wind.
- Gullies that might flood in a storm's flash flood.
- Still water that might harbor mosquitoes and other insects.

Good Sites

- Near good drinking water.
- Flat and level without big rocks or stumps.
- Well drained.
- Sheltered from the wind (unless you have to escape bugs.)
- Near sources of wood for fuel.
- Above high water mark if near rivers/lakes/oceans.

TIPS FOR THE TRAIL

How to Make Soap

1. Melt animal fat over the fire and pour into a container.
2. Mix water with ashes from fire and strain the liquid into a jar.
3. Over fire, mix two parts fat with one part liquid from step (2) above (this is potash or lye) and boil until it thickens. After cooling, use the liquid directly, or pour into a pan to harden.

TIPS FOR THE TRAIL

Leave No Trace - Seven Principles

❶ Plan ahead and prepare

- Know the regulations and special concerns for the area you'll visit.
- Prepare for extreme weather, hazards, and emergencies.
- Schedule your trip to avoid times of high use.
- Visit in small groups. Split larger parties into groups of 4-6.
- Repackage food to minimize waste.
- Use a map and compass to eliminate the use of marking paint, rock cairns or flagging.

❷ Travel and camp on durable surfaces

- Durable surfaces include established trails and campsites, rock, gravel, dry grasses or snow.
- Protect riparian areas by camping at least 200 feet from lakes and streams.
- Good campsites are found, not made. Altering a site is not necessary.

In popular areas---

- Concentrate use on existing trails and campsites.
- Walk single file in the middle of the trail, even when wet or muddy.
- Keep campsites small. Focus activity in areas where vegetation is absent.

In pristine areas---

- Disperse use to prevent the creation of campsites and trails.
- Avoid places where impacts are just beginning.

❸ Dispose of Waste Properly

- Pack it in, pack it out. Inspect your campsite and rest areas for trash or spilled foods. Pack out all trash, leftover food, and litter.
- Deposit solid human waste in cat holes dug 6 to 8 inches deep at least 200 feet from water, camp, and trails. Cover and disguise the cat hole when finished.
- Pack out toilet paper and hygiene products.
- To wash yourself or your dishes, carry water 200 feet away from streams or lakes and use small amounts of biodegradable soap. Scatter strained dishwater.

TIPS FOR THE TRAIL

Leave No Trace (continued)

❹ Leave What You Find

- Preserve the past: examine, but do not touch, cultural or historic structures and artifacts.
- Leave rocks, plants and other natural objects as you find them.
- Avoid introducing or transporting non-native species.
- Do not build structures, furniture, or dig trenches.

❺ Minimize Campfire Impacts

- Campfires can cause lasting impacts to the backcountry. Use a lightweight stove for cooking and enjoy a candle lantern for light.
- Where fires are permitted, use established fire rings, fire pans, or mound fires.
- Keep fires small. Only use sticks from the ground that can be broken by hand.
- Burn all wood and coals to ash, put out campfires completely, then scatter cool ashes.

❻ Respect Wildlife

- Observe wildlife from a distance. Do not follow or approach them.
- Never feed animals. Feeding wildlife damages their health, alters natural behaviors, and exposes them to predators and other dangers.
- Protect wildlife and your food by storing rations and trash securely.
- Control pets at all times, or leave them at home.
- Avoid wildlife during sensitive times: mating, nesting, raising young, or winter.

❼ Be Considerate of Other Visitors

- Respect other visitors and protect the quality of their experience.
- Be courteous. Yield to other users on the trail.
- Step to the downhill side of the trail when encountering pack stock.
- Take breaks and camp away from trails and other visitors.
- Let nature's sounds prevail. Avoid loud voices and noises.

Source: Leave No Trace Center for Outdoor Ethics

TIPS FOR THE TRAIL

Poker - Order of Hands from High to Low

All suits are equal in this ranking.

1. **Five of a Kind:** Five cards of the same rank. Only possible if you are using wild cards.
2. **Straight Flush**: Five cards of the same suit in sequence, such as **5-6-7-8-9**. The highest top card wins. Ace can be high or low. **A-K-Q-J-10** of the same suit is known as a Royal Flush and is the highest regular hand.
3. **Four of a kind:** Four cards of the same rank, such as **6-6-6-6**.
4. **Full House:** Three cards of one rank and two cards of another rank, such as **J-J-J-4-4**. The hand with the highest rank of three cards wins.
5. **Flush:** Five cards of the same suit in any sequence, such as **2-5-7-9-J** of clubs. The highest card wins. If the top cards are equal, compare the next card and so on.
6. **Straight:** Five cards of different suits in sequence, such as **7-8-9-10-J** of different suits. The straight with the highest top card wins. Ace can be high or low.
7. **Three of a Kind:** Three cards of the same rank, such as **J-J-J**. The highest ranking wins.
8. **Two Pairs:** Two sets of 2 cards of the same rank, such as **5-5-Q-Q**. The highest pair wins. If they are equal, compare the next pair, then the remaining card.
9. **One Pair:** 2 cards of the same rank, such as **8-8**. The highest pair wins. If the pairs are equal, compare the next highest card, and so on.
10. **High Card:** If no matches, then the highest card wins. If they are equal, compare the next card, and so on.

TIPS FOR THE TRAIL

Navigation - Determining Distance Across River

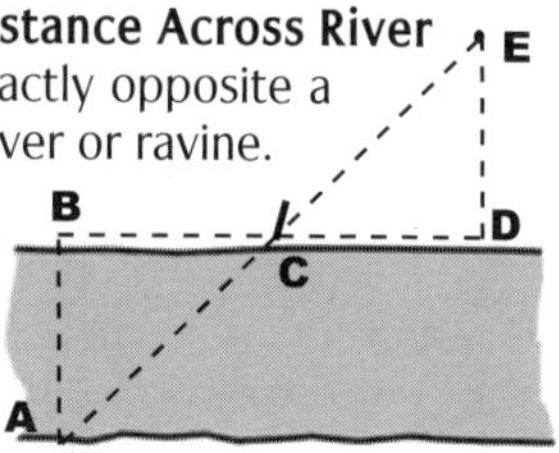

1. Pick out a point B that is exactly opposite a visible object A across the river or ravine.
2. Walk at right angles 20 feet or so to point C and place a stick in the ground.
3. Continue on the same path the exact same distance until you come to point D and mark that spot(BC=CD).
4. At D, turn at right angles and walk away from the river until you can line up the stick at point C with the object at A. Mark this spot E.
5. Distance D-E equals the distance across the river, A-B.

INDEX

TITLES, AUTHORS AND TIPS

TIPS FOR THE TRAIL

First Aid - Ticks

- Avoid ticks in the first place. Stay on trails, avoid tall vegatation. Wear light colored clothes so the ticks can be seen. Wear long sleeve shirts and pants and tuck the pants into your socks. Wear a hat. If you must wear shorts, wear gaiters as well.
- Check yourself (or have someone else check you) daily. Removing ticks within the first 36 hours is critical in preventing Lyme disease.
- **DO NOT** use heat or suffocation methods as these may cause the tick to release infecting bacteria.
- **DO** use tweezers to grab the tick as close to the skin as possible and pull gently straight out. Do not squeeze, twist or bend the tick.
- After removing the tick, clean the area with soap and/or alcohol and apply an antibiotic ointment.
- Place the tick in a plastic bag to take to your doctor if you are afraid of Lyme Disease. Also contact a doctor if you develop a 1" rash around the bite, or if you experience flu-like symptoms up to a month after a tick bite.
- If you have pets, be sure to carry out these same procedure on them.

TIPS FOR THE TRAIL

Cooking -- Measurement Conversions

1 km	= 1000 m	= .62 mile	= 3281 ft
1 meter	= 100 cm	= 39.37 in	
1 cm	= 10 mm	= .394 in	
1 mm	= .039 in		
1 mile	= 1760 yds	= 5280 ft	= 1.61 km
1 sq. mile	= 640 acres		
1 yard	= 3 ft	= 36 in	= .914 m
1 ft	= 12 in	= 30.48 cm	
1 in	= 2.54 cm	= 25.4 mm	
1 gallon	= 4 qts	= 128 oz	
1 qt	= 2 pints	= 4 cups	= .94 liter
1 pint	= 2 cups	= 16 oz	
1 cup	= 16 tbsp	= 8 oz	
1 tbsp	= 3 tsp	= 1/2 oz	
1 oz	= 2 tbsp	= 6 tsp	= 29.57 ml
1 pound	= 16 oz		
1 ton	= 2000 lb		
1 kg	= 1000 gm	= 2.54 lb	

$F^\circ = (9/5 * C^\circ) + 32$ $C^\circ = 5/9 * (F^\circ - 32)$